D1058396

CHINA'S RED REBEL

THE STORY OF
MAO TSE-TUNG

I.G. Edmonds

CHINA'S
RED REBEL

THE STORY OF
MAO TSE-TUNG

MACRAE SMITH COMPANY
Philadelphia

Library of Congress Cataloging in Publication Data

Edmonds, I   G
    China's red rebel

    Bibliography: p.
    SUMMARY: A biography of the ruler of a quarter of the earth's people
and leader of a country with nuclear power capability and veto power in the
United Nations Security Council.
    1. Mao, Tsê-tung, 1893-   —Juvenile literature.
[1. Mao, Tsê-tung, 1893-   2. China (People's Republic of China,
1949-   )—History] I. Title.
DS778.M3E35   951.05'092'4 [B] [92]   73-11246
ISBN O-8255-3017-2

iv

Contents

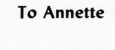

To Annette

Introduction

If all the world's people were assembled and the name of Mao Tse-tung should be flung at them, one-quarter would bow in veneration, one quarter would grimace in hate, and another quarter would receive the name with respect. The remaining quarter, from primitive civilizations of the world, probably have never heard of him.

A majority of people in the United States would probably fall into the category of those who are suspicious of this un-disputed giant of modern China. Mao represents an ideology at odds with the American economic and political systems. His forces in the Chinese civil war displaced a major U.S. political ally, Chiang Kai-shek, now of Taiwan. Mao then led his nation in a war in Korea against United Nations forces where the bulk of the fighting fell upon troops of the United States. Again in Vietnam Mao's government chose to support a people fighting against the United States and her South Vietnam friends.

1

Whether or not Mao needed to be considered an enemy to the United States is a political question that pundits fail to agree on. But the hostile viewpoint of a large segment of the United States has served to hide Mao's greatness from a lot of people. Greatness does not necessarily imply goodness or badness. A great man is one whose actions and beliefs affect the entire world and all the people in it.

Today Mao Tse-tung is the ruler of a quarter of the earth's people. His country possess a nuclear warfare capability. It is one of the five countries on earth powerful enough to hold a veto power in the United Nations Security Council. Such a man and leader cannot be ignored.

There is no doubt that much of the trouble between Red China and the United States in recent years was due to lack of understanding. Certainly no one can understand the People's Republic of China today without an understanding of Mao Tse-tung and what he stands for. Mao created Red China and made it into the superpower it is today. An understanding of Mao Tse-tung is necessary to get along with his country's newly emerging political power. An understanding of him would be necessary also for any nation that might choose not to get along with Mao's China, for there is a Chinese proverb to the effect that one must know his enemy well before one can hope to destroy that enemy.

That, then, is the purpose of this book: to provide an understanding of one of the most influential men of the twentieth century. It is not a book that intends to make a hero of Mao; nor is its purpose to make a villain of him, but rather to present the facts of his life as they intertwine in the world-shaking events that changed China from a broken shell to a superpower with a corresponding influence upon the lives of all of us in the world.

The image of Mao is shadowy. It merges into the events of his time so that it is difficult to get a continually clear view of the man himself. There have been several biographies and numerous books about his accomplishments in the rise of

Red China. They all suffer from gaps and from incorrect information.

There is no doubt that at the time they were written they were based upon the best research available. However, the changing times have disclosed additional information that reveals past mistakes in Mao's biographies.

In one case the author said that Mao dominated the Communist Party in China from 1929 on. New research shows that he did not gain control until 1935, and even then his grip was precarious. Another author referred to Mao as the "undisputed ruler of Red China" at a time when he was actually a prisoner of the ruling clique and, by Mao's own admission later, was not consulted on any major issue for six years. Another case in point is the declaration in one book that Mao's greatest supporter was a man who in fact proved to be even then plotting Mao's murder to further his own ambitions.

Thus new information permits a biographer to bring a little more of the real Mao Tse-tung out of the shadows. What comes out is neither all good nor all bad, and that is as it should be, for it is the way men are.

1
Young Rebel

They say that Mao Jen-sheng was a tall man who carried himself very erect, as became an old soldier. He was spare of flesh and his wispy beard hung below a petulant mouth that seemed ready to express nothing except condemnation of all he saw and heard. His eyes were especially harsh. They regarded all the world as his enemy, including his skinny first son, Mao Jun-chih, who would later be known as Mao Tse-tung.

The elder Mao never recovered from the effects of a bitter childhood and an unhappy adolescence. His family had been poor peasants but better off than most, for they at least owned their tiny plot of ground. In time Jen-sheng's father and grandfather died, leaving debts the teen-age boy was unable to pay. He struggled along for a year on the farm before he was forced to deed over the precious land to meet the old debts. The boy then sold himself into the service of a warlord for a bit of money to keep his mother from starving.

4

Those were the years during the last half of the nineteenth century when the Manchu dynasty, which had ruled China for the past 300 years, was crumbling. Foreign nations were hacking off huge chunks of Chinese territory and forcing the weakened nation to make humiliating concessions. Graft and corruption were rampant. In the army, everyone from generals to private soldiers thought only of what loot they could steal. It would appear that Mao's father happened on some kind of good fortune sometime in his army career, for he was able to return to his village and to redeem the lost family farm in the village of Shao Shan, forty miles south of Changsa, the capital of Hunam province, in southern China. Jen-sheng seems to have had a little money left over, for he soon began buying and speculating in rice, in addition to farming his own land.

Mao Jen-sheng then took a wife from a neighboring village. It was said by Emi Siao, who knew Mao, that the house strad-dled the dividing line of two farms. The Mao and Tcou families shared the common dwelling with the dividing line running through the guest room or parlor. It was made of mud bricks and thatched with rice straw. A wall surrounded the entire house, and there was a family courtyard in the rear.

Jen-sheng's new wife was as amiable as he was dour. She was stockily built, with a moon face that was said to be rather pretty. She was a hard-working woman but constantly infu-riated her husband by giving rice to beggars. Jen-sheng had worked hard all his life and saw no reason for giving any of his rice away.

Less than a year after the marriage, a son was born, the boy who would become Mao Tse-tung. It was said that the day of his birth was the first and last time any of the neighbors could recall seeing Jen-sheng smile. The birth of a first son was al-ways a joyous occasion in old China. "A man sees his im-mortality in the grandchildren playing around his door," a country proverb ran. The birth of a son insured Mao Jen-sheng a secure old age and remembrance after death, or so he thought then.

As it happened, father and son grew to hate each other. Just what soured the old soldier on his firstborn son remained his own secret. Mao Tse-tung himself never really knew. As far back as Mao can remember he lived in fear of his father's tongue and stick.

Jen-sheng's bitterness and hatred of the world in general increased with the years. This was strange, for he prospered more than his neighbors. He was a frugal man who worked his family hard, fed them just enough to live on, and sold the rest to increase his property. In time he was able to produce enough rice to be able to feed his family on half and have a full half to sell. At the same time he had sufficient cash on hand to buy grain from his neighbors to store until prices got better. Strangely, the father of the boy who would become one of the most famous Communists in history was an outstanding example of a capitalist.

Within a few years Jen-sheng was wealthy by peasant standards and the father of three sons and a daughter. This good fortune only increased the old man's bitterness. Robert Payne said, "Some secret anxiety gnawed in him; he was always restless, ill at ease, the hot temper never very far from the surface." Another writer has suggested that the old man's feeling may have been caused by something he did during his years as a soldier for the Manchus—perhaps it even had to do with the way he obtained the small money stake that permitted him to rebuy his family home.

Despite his father's cruelty, those childhood years were not especially unhappy for young Mao. He had few chores before he was six. He played with his brothers and learned to swim in the lake across from his home. The carefree days ended when he was seven. He then began to accompany the family to the rice fields. During the planting season, he helped pull rice seedlings from their beds. During the harvest he was too small to cut grain but helped glean the fields for any spilled grains of rice. During the growing season, his father perched Mao on a wicker stand to act as a human scarecrow to frighten away the paddy birds who flocked in to peck at the swelling rice heads.

The first great change in the boy's life came when his father sent him to primary school in their village. Mao was not a good scholar. His calligraphy (Chinese picture writing) remained clumsy all his life. However, he learned to read and to work the abacus, that primitive calculating machine. As soon as the boy could figure and write sufficiently, Jen-sheng put him to keeping books for his father's rice business.

About this time Mao discovered that there were other books besides the one his teacher forced him to pore over. These books were glorious tales of bandits and heroes who defied cruel officials just as he often defied his father. Mao was entranced. His learning had not progressed to the point where he could make out all the words, but he gathered enough to follow the trend of the plots.

One of these books was the fourteenth century novel *Water Margins Tale*, by Shih Nai-an. This book is best known to the West as *All Men Are Brothers*, a title given to it by Pearl S. Buck when she translated the classic into English in 1933. It is a bloodthirsty tale of a group of outlaws who represent a Chinese equivalent of Robin Hood. Some of the ideas in the book made a lasting impression on Mao. One story that was particularly appealing to him told how the hero Chih Chin tried to capture his enemies and persuade them to join him instead of fighting him. Later Mao did the same thing time and again as he struggled to build up the Chinese Communist Army.

The *Water Margins Tale* and other books like *The Three Kingdoms* and *The Dream of the Red Chamber* expanded the young boy's horizon, showing him that there was a greater world beyond the borders of Hunan, his native province.

Hunan means "South of the Lake." The name refers to the huge Tungting Lake on the plains in the northern section of

Hunan. The lake is fed by the Yangtze River. From the lake area the land rises in the east, west and south to rugged mountain ranges that have been hideouts for bandits from time immemorial.

One of the most famous of the mountain bandit areas was a particularly wild mass of volcanic rock called Chingkanshan near the Kiangsi-Fukien border. This famous mountain was so difficult to climb that a small force could hold it against great odds. As he grew up, Mao heard many tales about the bandits operating in that area. Sometimes in his play he prophetically pictured himself as a great bandit chief leading his forces down out of the wilds of Chingkanshan to attack rich officials.

Until he was six and started to the village school, Mao had dumbly followed his devout mother in attending the local Buddhist temple. He humbly bowed his shaven head with its thin queue hanging down his back as she ignited her prayer sticks and prayed for the welfare of her family. From his mother Mao also gained a deep respect for the Empress Dowager who ruled the empire in the name of her underage grandson.

Mao had a good reason to remember the empress because her birthday was the occasion for special celebrations in the temple courtyard. At that time there would be brightly colored lanterns, fireworks and laughter. One of these birthday celebrations was suddenly interrupted by soldiers who came marching through Shao Shan on their way to Changsha, the capital of Hunan. The village boys crowding the roadside to stare at the troops were captivated by the uniforms and guns. In the excitement they did not learn why the soldiers streamed down their road.

The reason, as Mao learned later from the guarded remarks of some men, was that the harvest had been poor that year throughout Hunan. A mob of starving people had petitioned the governor in Changsha for rice.

"Why haven't you food of your own?" he asked them. "I have plenty."

Infuriated by the governor's indifference, the mob broke

into his courtyard. They were driven back, but the frightened official rushed in new troops from the south to guard against any more uprisings.

News traveled slowly in China in 1904. Mao did not hear until later that a Hunanese student named Huang Hsing had chosen this same day, October 10, to begin a revolution he hoped would spread and overthrow the Manchu government in Peking.

Huang Hsing's first objective was Changsha. With the capital as a base, the young revolutionist hoped to gather support that would enable him to control all of Hunan. His next step would then be an assault on Peking. Hunan was selected for the initial phase of the revolt because the Hunanese people were notorious for their rebellious nature. A Chinese proverb claimed that their tempers were as hot as the peppers they grew.

Huang Hsing's revolt failed, partly because of the troops that had been pulled into Changsha to quell the food riots. Huang Hsing fled into the hills of Hunan like the bandit hero of *All Men Are Brothers*. Later he made his way to Japan, where he began plans for another revolt.

In later years Mao told the American journalist Edgar Snow that it was stories of Huang Hsing's revolt that first stirred his social consciousness and started him on the road to becoming a Communist.

Mao's next lesson in revolt came as a result of a violent quarrel with Mao Jen-sheng. This happened in 1906 when Mao was thirteen, but it was still as fresh as yesterday in Mao's mind when he told Edgar Snow about it in 1937.

"My father denounced me before the whole group [of guests]," Mao recalled, "calling me lazy and useless. This infuriated me. I cursed him and left the house."

Mao's mother, crying and wringing her hands, ran after her son. Mao Jen-sheng followed, screaming curses at the fleeing boy as he demanded that Mao return and kowtow; that is, to fall on his knees and bump his head on the ground in token of submission to his father. Mao kept running. His blue trouser legs flapped and his long queue (which the Manchu government required all Chinese to wear) stood out behind him.

He stopped only when he got to the brink of the small cliff overlooking the pond across the road from his house.

"I'll jump in! I'll drown myself!" he cried hysterically.

Mao Jen-sheng stopped, although he kept shouting and cursing at his son. He did not approach closer, however, for the wild hysteria in the boy's face frightened the old man. Mao Jen-sheng was convinced that Mao would kill himself if pressed.

For a time the two held their positions, screaming at each other. The guests, neighbors and people passing in the road stopped to watch the duel of wills between son and father. Mao Jen-sheng was caught in a position where stubbornness might cause the death of his son. On the other hand, if he gave in with so many people watching, he would lose face as a man who could not control his family.

For the first time, Mao realized that he had a weapon against his father's cruelty. He began bargaining. At the same time he was smart enough to know that he had to give in enough to salve his father's pride and to save the old man's face. Finally, in exchange for Mao's agreement to kowtow (but only on one bended knee), Mao Jen-sheng agreed not to beat the boy.

So they both won a victory. Mao's was the greater, for he had learned that he could stand up to his father. At that time Mao Jen-sheng represented oppression to the boy, but as Mao's world expanded and he learned there were other oppressors, he remembered how his father respected only those who fought him back. Ever after, Mao Tse-tung chose to fight rather than give in to those who oppressed or opposed him. Mao Tse-tung was not a born rebel. He was taught to be one by his strange, bitter father.

Everything that Mao broke with in Chinese tradition can be

traced back to his relations with Mao Jen-sheng. Subservience, the sanctity of the family unit, capitalism, and
time-honored customs all became hateful to the boy because
his father stood for those things. Under the influence of a different type of man, Mao Tse-tung would probably have
developed along an entirely different line, becoming a
scholarly teacher and poet of national stature.

Subservience and the sanctity of the family unit Mao rejected because he saw what a father's tyranny did not only to
himself but to his mother and brothers as well. Capitalism he
despised because he saw his father's warped greed. The Mao
family was adequately fed, but that was all. Mao recalled in
later life how Mao Jen-sheng would once a month provide an
egg with the rice given his hired hands. "But he never gave
me an egg or meat," Mao said. The family continued to eat
the simpliest of foods and to wear patched clothing long after
Jen-sheng had attained the status of a rich peasant. Every
available cent was put into expanding his rice brokerage
business and in buying up mortgages on farms.

As for his rejection of Chinese tradition and custom, we
have Mao's own comment that from early childhood one of his
ambitions was to burn down the temple to Confucius in his
home town. That was because from morning until night all he
heard from Mao Jen-sheng was one Confucian maxim after
another until the boy came to hate the very suggestion of
Confucius. After he began to study the Confucius *Analects* in
school, Mao found a weapon he could use against the old man.
When his father upbraided him with a quotation from Confucius about laziness, Mao would retort with an apt quotation on
the duties of a parent. And so on it went, two incompatible
people taking out their hate and spite on each other through
the words of the sage.

From all reports, Mao Jen-sheng certainly had reason to ac-
cuse his son of being unfilial, but his claims that Mao was lazy
were ill-founded. Mao worked hard, and his once frail body

filled out, building the firmness and strength that would be his salvation in later years.

To exemplify how much work Mao could do when he was of a mind for it, Siao-yu, who knew Mao as a young man, tells of the time Mao Jen-sheng caught his son behind a tomb reading a book when he should have been carrying manure to fertilize the fields. The boy protested that he had carried five loads and had stopped to rest. When the old man sneered at the idea of five loads as a day's work, Mao asked how many loads he was expected to carry in a day. Jen-sheng said fifteen. Mao nodded, put away his book and went back to work.

The next day the old man came spying on his son again and found Mao behind the tomb reading *The Three Kingdoms* for the twentieth time. Before the outraged man could denounce him again and begin spouting Confucianisms about laziness, Mao quickly pointed out that he had already carried his required fifteen loads. Jen-sheng checked and found that what Mao had said was true. In a half day he had done the work of two laborers.

Jen-sheng was almost beside himself with rage, but he could say nothing more. The hired man he kept had heard him tell Mao that fifteen loads was a day's work. He could not insist on his son's doing more without causing himself to lose face, so he went away, cursing and calling on heaven to witness the unfilial attitude of this despicable son his wife had cursed him with. Mao returned to his beloved book, doubly happy for having time to read and besting his father.

Another showdown between father and son came over the question of a wife for Mao. Mao Jen-sheng, like all Chinese of his generation, considered continuation of the family the primary objective of life. Whatever else happened, the line must go on or there would be no one to tend the graves and venerate the spirits of the fathers and grandfathers who had passed on.

As a result, as soon as Mao was physically able to father a

child Mao Jen-sheng picked him a wife. Only a passing mention of her has survived the memories of the years. Even her name has been lost, and whatever finally became of her is equally a mystery. She seems to have been a farmer's daughter from Siang-Siang, the area where Mao's mother came from. She was twenty years old, six years older than the very reluctant bridegroom.

Apparently there was a formal wedding in which the bride was carried to her new home in a sedan chair and all the ancient rituals were carried out. Mao Tse-tung later said, "I never considered myself married and I never lived with her," implying that there was a true marriage.

To a fourteen-year-old boy twenty is an ancient age, and Mao flatly refused to have anything to do with the "old woman" his father had picked for him. Jen-sheng looked upon his son's refusal to provide the family with grandsons as a direct attack upon the perpetuation of the family and an attempt to harm Jen-sheng's own spirit after the old man passed to the other world. No details of the titanic fight this caused has survived, but it apparently surpassed all the fights they had previously or would ever have again. Mao's attitude can be summed up in a proverbial folk saying that can be found expressed somehow in practically every country: "You can lead a horse to water, but you can't make him drink."

The stage was now set for the final big battle between father and son, the battle that would tear the boy's roots out of Shao Shan village and set his feet on the long march that would take him to a place among the immortals of China.

2
Schooldays

Mao Tse-tung left his native village when he was sixteen. He first went to the primary school in Siang-Siang, a town fifteen miles from Shao Shan. After a year there, he moved on to a school in Changsa, the capital of Hunan.

It was not easy to obtain Mao Jen-sheng's permission to leave home. Mao had become very valuable to the old man both as an accountant to keep book on the rice broker business and as a field hand in between. The old man considered the brief schooling Mao had gotten in Shao Shan to be sufficient for running the rice and farm business which Mao, as the oldest son, would inherit when Jen-sheng became too old to work.

In this battle Mao had the detested Confucius on his side. Mao Jen-sheng just could not find any of the ancient sage's wisdom that would refute a boy's desire to be educated, so the old man finally gave his consent.

It is part of the legend of Mao Tse-tung that Jen-sheng had

refused him permission to leave because he needed Mao to work in the fields, and that Mao then borrowed twelve dollars (a year's salary for a field coolie) and gave the money to his father. It makes a good story and has been repeated endlessly. Perhaps it happened, but it seems odd that Jen-sheng should have required his son to hire his own replacement and then provided Mao with an allowance, for he several times threatened to cut it off when Mao displeased him.

Siao-Yu, a friend who later turned against Mao, has left a detailed story of Mao's journey to school. Siao-Yu did not actually meet Mao until a year after this, but presumably he got the details from his brother Emi Siao or from Mao.

Mao left home in the fall of 1909. His father ignored his departure, but his mother came with him to the courtyard gate, gently inquiring if he had all he needed. He had rolled a blue mosquito net, two old sheets, two extra tunics and an extra pair of pants into a bundle that he carried over his shoulder at one end of a carry-pole. The other end of the pole was balanced with worn copies of his precious books *Romance of the Three Kingdoms* and *Water Margins Tale*.

It was fifteen miles to the Tungshan Primary School in Siang-Siang. Mao soon joined another group going to the school, although Siao-Yu indicates that he wasn't particularly welcome. However, he was now tall and sturdy, and the others did not want to offend him.

Tungshan was a small school in a small town, but both seemed enormous to the boy. He had never been beyond his little village before. Siao-Yu drew a picture of the place for his book *Mao Tse-Tung and I were Beggars*. It shows a tree-lined moat spanned by a stone bridge. In the background is a fifteen-foot-high wall pierced by a single gate. It looks like a fortress, and Siao-Yu said the students referred to it as the "Great Wall of China."

In telling his life story to Edgar Snow, Mao had little to say about his half year at Tungshan. He chiefly remembered how he was sneered at by sons of rich parents because of his poor clothes and rustic manners. Mao did not mention any difficulty in enrolling in the school.

Siao-Yu tells a different story. He claimed that Mao was turned down by the headmaster because he was too big to go to school with the smaller children and because two years of schooling in his village was not sufficient preparation for Tungshan.

Mao pleaded for a chance to try, but the headmaster again refused. Just as Mao was in despair at the thought of having to return home to face his father's jeers, a teacher named Hu interceded for him. Hu proposed that they give Mao a chance to prove himself. The headmaster agreed to a five months' trial period and charged Mao 1,400 copper coins for tuition and board.

All who have written about Mao agree that the force of his personality soon overcame the contempt of his fellow students. His particular friend was the elegant son of a rich farmer. This boy, who was two years younger than Mao, was named Siao Chu-chang. He was the brother of Siao-Yu, with whom Mao Tse-tung would be associated later. Siao Chu-chang was known to Mao as Siao San or Siao the Third because he was a third son. In later years, Siao San became enamored of the writings of Rousseau and called himself "Emi Siao" after the character Emil in the Frenchman's novel of that name. He dropped the "l" from the name because it was difficult for Chinese to pronounce. In time, Siao-Yu rejected communism and also his brother and his old friend Mao Tse-tung. Emi Siao eventually went to Russia, where he gained fame as a translator of Chinese poetry into Russian. He also wrote a book about Mao, which was published in Bombay in 1955 under the title *Mao Tse-tung, His Childhood and Youth.*

Emi Siao, as we shall call him, since he is best known by that name, was a great influence in expanding Mao Tse-tung's narrow view of the world. The school in Shao Shan had been a classical school in the old Chinese scholarship tradition. The students were trained in reading the classics and in writing essays in the classical style, with emphasis on beautiful calligraphy. There was little in their studies that concerned the world about them.

The riots and Huang Hsing's attempt at revolt had shown the rebellious boy that there was more to the world than his own village. He wanted to attend Tungshan because he had heard that it was a modern school that based its teachings on an awareness of life today rather than the traditional world of Confucius. As a result, Mao absorbed everything new as readily as a dry sponge soaks up water. His new friend Emi Siao had a wide knowledge of history and geography, and Mao learned much from him long before his new teachers got around to their own explanations.

Although the students were paying guests, they still had school chores and clean-up duties to perform. During the class day, there were breaks when they went out in groups to sweep the yards, clean up leaves, and keep the place presentable. During those sessions away from their books, Mao worked alongside Emi Siao, listening avidly as the younger boy talked of strange places and wonders beyond anything the boy from Shao Shan had ever dreamed of. It was during these conversations that Mao's future greatness first began to show through the veneer of his ignorance. He was not content merely to listen. He questioned, probed for additional information, and finally drew his own conclusions rather than accept those handed to him. Years later this same characteristic would be the root of his rejection of Stalinist communism and the cause of today's split between Russia and China.

The young man's ideas were further expanded by a teacher who took part of each study day to tell them about conditions in China. Bitterly he told the students about how "foreign devils" were slowly cutting China to pieces. It was during such a lecture that Mao learned for the first time that the emperor, who had succeeded the Empress Dowager Tzu Hsi after her death in 1908, was an interloper and not Chinese at all. He was a Manchu, a member of the race that conquered China in the seventeenth century.

In 1644 the weak Ming dynasty of China had asked the Manchus of Manchuria to help defend China against the marauding Tartars. The Manchus drove back the invaders but remained to conquer China themselves. As the years passed, the warlike spirit of the Manchus gradually decayed. Foreigners forced the emperor to permit them to trade in China.

At first the traders were restricted to a single port. That restriction ended in 1840, when Great Britain declared war because the Chinese government tried to prevent British traders from importing opium into China. In 1856, another war with Great Britain forced China to make additional concessions. This was followed in 1885 by French agressions in Indochina, and in 1894 by the Sino-Japanese War, which ended Chinese control of Formosa and Korea. Then the Russians tried to seize Manchuria but had to retreat in the face of Japanese displeasure. Japan had her own designs on that Chinese province.

At the same time rapacious foreign governments were cutting China to pieces, the country's social conditions were intolerable. The lives of coolies in the cities were subhuman. The peasants were equally oppressed, with absentee landlords taking as much as seventy percent of their crops. What was left was usually insufficient to feed a family through the winter. Thousands starved throughout China. The Mao family, since they owned their own land, escaped this calamity. Now Mao learned that the food riots of Changsa, which had disturbed him when he was eleven, were common all through China.

The country was ripe for revolution but lacked the right kind of leadership to bring it about. In 1850 a religious fanatic named Hung Hsiu-chuan led what became known to Chinese history as the Taiping Rebellion. Hung captured Nanking, set up his own dynasty, and came close to capturing Peking itself before his revolt was crushed by a Manchu army partly commanded by American and British Army officers.

The continued decay of the Manchu government alarmed many young intellectuals, who decided that a republican form of government was China's only hope. One of the major leaders of the reform movement was Dr. Sun Yat-sen, who had been forced to flee from China to escape execution by the strongly reactionary Empress Dowager. Tzu Hsi ruled China through puppets, whom she placed on the Manchu "peacock throne." Several times men working for Dr. Sun had launched revolts. All had been put down, but it thrilled Mao to learn that men were working to bring about revolution in China.

These stories completely changed his attitude of reverence toward China's rulers. He joined a group of boys who were equally outraged at the way the Manchus were permitting foreigners to slice away at China's territory. They pledged to cut off their queues (pigtail hair), since wearing the queue had been forced on the Chinese by their conquerors in 1644 as a mark of servility to the new government. Mao was the first to cut his off. Then when some of the boys lost their courage and refused to follow suit, he—being the largest boy in the school—threw them down and cut off their queues himself.

There is no record of what his teachers thought of this high-handedness. It is doubtful if they approved, although they had a reputation of running a modern school. Some of the boys involved came from influential families in Siang-Siang.

There is a story related by Siao-Yu that also indicates that reports that Mao Tse-tung was well liked by his teachers may be something of an exaggeration. Apparently he was as bull-headed and rebellious at Tungshan as he had been at home. Ever since he had been introduced to the *Romance of the Three Kingdoms* by his teacher in Shao Shan, Mao had revered the book and its characters. He accepted every word as history and read and reread the book. A tattered copy was one of the few possessions he brought to Tungshan with him.

One day he was startled in class to hear his history teacher say that the book was a novel. While the story was based upon facts, the author had changed events and situations to fit his plot. Mao became violently indignant.

Siao-Yu wrote, "He became more stubborn . . . He even went so far as to suggest to his schoolmates that they start a movement to get rid of the teacher." The headmaster tried to reason with Mao when the history teacher failed. Mao insisted to the other boys that the headmaster was trying to protect the history teacher because they were cousins. "He even produced a petition addressed to the mayor of the city asking that the headmaster be replaced, and he urged all the students to sign it. When no one would sign, Mao was furious," Siao-Yu wrote.

Mao's schooling at Tungshan ended at the conclusion of the five-month probationary period. Other biographers suggest that Mao was simply looking for a more advanced school. Siao-Yu's account indicates that Mao was no longer welcome. In fact, after this fight over the *Romance of the Three Kingdoms,* the rest of the boys became afraid of him. Only Emi Siao remained his friend. Siao-Yu, the other brother, was not at Tungshan at this time but had moved to Changsha's school the previous year.

Before Mao left Tungshan he read a book lent him by Emi Siao. It was called *Great Heroes of the World.* It had been translated into Chinese and contained stories about George Washington, Peter the Great of Russia, Lord Wellington of Great Britain, Abraham Lincoln and other famous people. Mao was fascinated by the book and almost ruined it by underscoring passages with his writing brush. This book was the first place Mao had ever heard of the United States. The story of George Washington's revolutionary trials made a deep impression on him. Each of the persons included in the book had been able in different ages to protect his country from foreign aggression. Thinking of the way China was being dismembered by Russia, France, England, and Japan, Mao told Emi Siao: "We need great men like these. We ought to study them and find out how we can make China rich and strong, and so avoid becoming like Annam, Korea and India [that is, countries that have been taken over by foreign nations]."

This report comes from Emi Siao's account. Later Robert Payne, the American writer, talked to Emi Siao and asked about this particular point. At that time Emi Siao told Payne: "It was all very strange. I can remember exactly how [Mao] looked, and I can remember his tone as he said 'We need great people like these.' I had the feeling that he had made his decision . . . He breathed authority."

On this evidence we can conclude that Mao Tse-tung was still only sixteen years old when he made his decision to turn his naturally rebellious spirit to fighting for China. The combination of what he had learned from Emi Siao, from his teachers' talk of China's peril, and from the book *Great Heroes of the World* had given him a new goal in life. Instead of the scholarly teacher he had previously pictured himself to be, he would become the savior of China as Washington had saved the American colonies, as Wellington had saved England, as Catherine the Great had preserved Russia, and as Napoleon came onstage at a moment of French crisis to save his country.

Although he had picked his goal, Mao still lacked direction. He was sixteen years old and his schooling totaled only about three formal years. While he had read widely, he had not read wisely. As a result there were great gaps in his knowledge. He had never heard of either socialism or communism. If he had any political position at sixteen, it was that of "reformist." He believed that the government of China must be replaced. His individual heroes of the moment were Kang Yu-wei and Hung Hsiu-chuan of the Taipings. Kang Yu-wei in 1897 had managed to gain the confidence of Emperor Kuang Hsu and persuaded the young ruler to make some reforms. These had been cut short by the violently reactionary Empress Dowager who had put Kuang Hsu, her nephew, on the throne. She then banished the reformers and forced the emperor to sign documents that virtually transferred imperial power to her. At this stage Mao did not clearly understand what Kang Yu-wei stood for. He only knew that Kang's program promised reforms and changes.

He understood even less the true character of Hung Hsiu-chuan of the Taipings. Hung studied just enough under foreign missionaries to get a distorted view of Christianity. Then he had a vision in which an angel came down from heaven, cut open his belly, and replaced all his vital organs with substitutes brought from the sky. This made him a son of heaven and he began preaching to an increasing number of converts. They finally grew so large that he was able to launch a revolution that came close to succeeding. But as he gained power, Hung Hsiu-chuan made himself an emperor. In the end his new dynasty was destroyed. The remnants of his forces retreated across China and were finally destroyed completely in a dramatic battle along the Tatu River Gorge near the border of Tibet.

Mao had his seventeenth birthday at Tungshan. Then in the spring he either was asked to leave or decided to leave of his own accord. Fifteen-year-old Emi Siao went with him. They went first to Siangtan, upriver from Siang-Siang, but when Mao was refused admission at the local school they went on to Changsha, the provincial capital.

Mao told Edgar Snow: "I walked to Changsha . . . hardly daring to hope I could actually become a student in this great school. To my astonishment, I was admitted without difficulty."

Emi Siao tells a different story. He says they went by river boat down the Siang River but agrees that they were accepted by the Changsha school without trouble. This was possibly owing to help from Siao-Yu, who was a student at the Changsha Normal School across town. The older Siao brother was well liked by his teachers and possibly asked them to intercede with the lower school to help his brother Emi and his friend Mao Tse-tung.

For the first time in his life Mao was truly happy. He was thrilled by the big city and utterly delighted with the school library. He attached his studies with an enthusiasm that soon made him one of the top students. Later one of his professors said that of all the students he had taught during his long teaching career, Siao-Yu, Tsai Hosen (one of Mao's friends) and Mao Tse-tung stood out as the best of them all.

Mao, however, did not have much opportunity to get really deep into the academic life. He and Emi Siao arrived in Changsha in the early summer of 1911. In October of that year the long-delayed revolution finally exploded. The revolt began on October 19, 1911, sparked by a railroad strike in Szechuan Province. Imperial troops were rushed to Szechuan to help provincial authorities put down the disturbance. Dr. Sun Yat-sen's revolutionary group worked feverishly to support the strikers and to spread the disturbance. For the first time in modern Chinese revolutionary history, all rebel groups put aside their differences and pulled together. A rash of insurrections swept across the country. The revolution swept from one victory to another. Manchu resistance crumbled, and by February, 1912, the frightened Imperial regent signed an abdication proclamation for the boy-emperor Pu-yi, who had succeeded his venerable aunt the Empress Dowager. A provisional government was hastily formed, with Dr. Sun Yat-sen as the head of the governing tribunal.

Like most of China's youth, Mao Tse-tung was swept up by the excitement. A military command was formed at his school immediately after the revolution began. Mao refused to join. With a few friends, he left for Wuchang to join the rebel army. They arrived too late for the fighting, however, and returned to Changsha. By that time the New Model Army, the revolutionary group, had marched into the city and the governor had surrendered.

Mao then joined the revolutionary army. It was not a happy experience for him. He was a born leader and found it difficult at that time to be a follower. The main thing he got from his army experience was an understanding of the common soldier's viewpoint. This influenced him later when he led his own armies. Mao did not become involved in the fighting at that time. His work was divided between basic military training and acting as a servant for his company's officers.

His pay was seven dollars a month. Two dollars of it he spent for food, since the army mess was poor. The rest Mao saved, except for what he spent for newspapers. He saw his first newspaper when he came to Changsha, and for the rest of his life he remained an avid reader. Emi Siao claims that newspapers were what led Mao into his first true social awareness. Before, he had realized the need for reform and solidly backed the reform movement without actually knowing what the movement stood for. His newspaper reading while in the army gave him his first clear view of wide social conditions and current thought on their solution.

The thing that electrified the eighteen-year-old was an article on socialism. Realizing that reform was needed, he had not understood how reform could be carried out. The idea of collective ownership by the people of a nation's production so thrilled Mao that he immediately wrote letters to his friends back in Tungshan telling them what he had learned.

His interest in socialism was shortlived. Not long after that, he heard of communism from his friend Tsai Ho-chen, an ardent believer in Karl Marx. Mao was greatly interested in this philosophy. It seemed to go far beyond socialism in advocating ownership by the state, which, in turn, the people controlled. He wanted to know more about it, but his military duties left him scant time to study. By that time, many of his illiterate officers had discovered that Mao could write, and they used him to do their letters and reports. Literacy among the common soldiers was rare at that time.

Fortunately for Mao, the revolution ended quickly. The Manchu government, seeing its armies collapse before the onslaught of the rebels, recalled its disgraced former prime minister Yuan Shih-kai to command the imperial army. Yuan had been implicated in an earlier attempt to overthrow the imperial dynasty. However, the frightened prince regent had no choice but to recall Yuan from Manchurian exile. He was the only available leader strong enough to rally the army against Sun Yat-sen's successful rebels.

Even more important, Yuan Shih-kai had the confidence of the foreign colony in China. The Manchu government hoped that Yuan might be able to obtain military aid from France, England, Russia or Japan to destroy Sun Yat-sen.

Dr. Sun realized the danger to his revolution. He knew he could not possibly unite the badly divided country very quickly. He desperately feared foreign intervention. He had obtained a pledge from England and Japan not to support the Manchus, but he was sure that France would gladly intervene as an excuse to seize more Chinese territory to add to her holdings in Indochina.

After much agonizing analysis of his own shaky position as provisional president of a republic he had not yet conquered, Sun decided to make his own deal with Yuan Shih-kai. Robert Payne called Sun's decision "inexplicable," but the reason is clear enough. Sun realized that his revolt would fail if France came to Yuan's aid, so he took the only way out. He offered Yuan the presidency of the new republic.

Yuan also knew that he could not put down the revolt without foreign aid, which he did not want to accept. He quickly accepted Sun Yat-sen's offer, which brought the fighting to an end.

Sun thought he could use Yuan Shih-kai to bring peace and stability to the new republic. Then Sun thought he could shove Yuan aside. Yuan, in turn, had his own crafty plans. He intended to use Sun Yat-sen to stop the rebel fighting. Then Yuan intended to abolish the republic and make himself emperor.

Meanwhile, Private Mao Tse-tung, serving his officers, was totally unaware of this backstage maneuvering, or that they would set off a chain of events that would swing him eventually into the mainstream with a starring role in world-shaking events.

3
In Search of Himself

Mao was demobilized in late 1912. He spent a few months at Changsha's Middle School but was dissatisfied with his teachers. His father, infuriated when Mao joined the army, had cut off the allowance he had sent his son while Mao was in school. The money Mao had saved from his seven-dollar-a-month Army salary was used up very quickly. He then faced the alternative of finding a job or returning to the farm to bow to Mao Jen-sheng's tyranny.

The problem was that he was untrained for anything except farming. This left nothing open to him except coolie labor if he chose not to return to Shao Shan. He was determined to starve before he would go home to face his father's sneers at his failure. He did, however, unbend to the point of asking Jen-sheng for help. Mao had seen an ad in a Changsha paper for some trade schools. He decided that one for soapmaking offered the best opportunity. He had no money for registration and wrote Jen-sheng. The old man, praising heaven that his wastrel son was at last showing some sense, supplied the money. Mao enrolled but was disconcerted to learn that the course was underwritten by a foreign missionary group who conducted all instruction in English. He was totally unable to comprehend the instructor and dropped out.

At this, the lowest ebb of his life, the Siao brothers came to his aid. They were able to get him enrolled in the newly formed Changsha Fourth Normal School. Tuition and board were free, but the extra money allowance formerly given students training to be teachers had been cut off by the new republican government. Emi Siao loaned Mao money in the beginning. Shortly after this, the Changsha Fourth Normal School was combined with the Changsha First Normal. Siao-Yu said that it was easy to pick out which students came from which school, because those of the First Normal had uniforms and those of the Fourth came from poor families. They wore what they had.

Siao-Yu was two grades ahead of Mao, although they were the same age. Emi Siao was a grade behind Mao. As a result Mao looked to Siao-Yu for help in his studies. The Siao brothers were not close. Later, when each went separate political ways, they never spoke or corresponded with each other for the rest of Siao-Yu's life.

Mao now thought that he had found his ultimate goal in life. He loved his studies and college life. He decided he would be a teacher, with the goal of someday becoming president of a great university.

At least this was the outward impression he gave his friends. There is one incident from this period of his life that showed he may have had dreams of climbing even higher. One evening soon after Yuah Shih-kai became president of the Republic of China on Sun Yat-sen's invitation, Mao was listening to his college friends as they discussed the new republic. Up to that point Mao had not even known what a republic was. He became very excited when he learned that there were such things as elected officials in that kind of government. He bombarded his friends with hundreds of questions about a republican government and how it worked. He asked if elections for head of state were like the old classical Chinese examinations for the Imperial civil service; that is, could any person compete? Mao became very thoughtful after being told that in theory this was so. In retrospect, it later seemed clear to those who were there at the time that Mao saw himself as a possible presidential candidate someday, just as earlier he had identified himself with the Western heroes who fought for freedom in their countries.

It quickly became apparent, however, that China was a republic in name only. Sun Yat-sen had supported Yuan Shih-kai as president, but Yuan used his new position to smash Sun's revolutionary party. Yuan ruled as a warlord as he consolidated his military position in preparation for a restoration of the monarchy with himself as emperor.

Mao was extremely busy. He had his school classes until four o'clock each day. Then he worked in the school library as an assistant until closing time. Sundays were free, and Mao and his friends liked to take long, strenuous walks into the hills beyond Changsha. They talked, argued, and composed extemporaneous poems as they trudged along the hilly trails.

For Mao this activity was a carry-over from his Tungshan days. Then he and Emi Siao had often wandered through the hills. On those jaunts Mao stripped to the waist even in the worst weather and marched along nearly naked on good days. He had become a physical culture faddist and believed he was soaking up life and energy with the sun. Indirectly those mountain walking trips would change the history of China, for they built into Mao's sturdy frame the stamina and strength that permitted him to survive the five "extermination" campaigns the Nationalist Chinese government eventually launched against him and the communist movement.

Siao-Yu tells how he and Mao would often collaborate on a poem as they were inspired by the beautiful scenery along the banks of the Siang River during those Sunday hikes. Siao-Yu or Mao would be struck with inspiration. He would call out a line or a verse. Then the other would pick up the thread and weave some more words. When he was out of ideas, the other would take over. Mao was developing into a poet of considerable ability.

Siao-Yu also left a description of Mao in those days: "His face was rather large, but his eyes were neither large nor penetrating . . . His nose was flattish and of a typical Chinese shape. His ears were well proportioned; his mouth quite small; his teeth very white and even. These good teeth helped to make his smile quite charming, so that no one would imagine that he was not genuinely sincere."

Siao-Yu described Mao as walking slowly and said that he was not a good speaker. These things may have been true in 1913, but men who knew Mao later spoke of his hurried, loping walk, and he became a hypnotic speaker whose clear logic was difficult to refute or to resist.

Emi Siao claims that Mao was generally a poor student. Essay writing, with its argumentive approach, appealed to Mao's rebellious spirit and he did so well in his classical essay writings that his teachers were willing to overlook his poor mathematics, his total failure in foreign languages, and his inability to master the art of beautiful calligraphy. Both Emi Siao and Edgar Snow tell about Mao's attitude toward classes he did not like. Drawing was one of the things he detested. Once, given an assignment to draw some common object, he scrawled a circle on his paper, labeled it an egg, and turned it in as his assignment.

In 1914 two major events happened in Mao's life. One was the outbreak of war in Europe. The other was the formation by Siao-Yu and himself of the Hsin Min Study Association.

Mao was not directly involved in the war, but he took an uncommon interest in it. He devoured every newspaper and magazine article he could get about the European struggle. He ransacked the university library for books on military strategy so he could follow the ideas behind the fluctuating battle lines in France. It was said that by the end of the war he knew as much about basic military strategy as any formal military academy graduate.

Just why he should take such an inordinate interest in military tactics and strategy was a mystery to his friends. They knew he had detested his months in the army. Under Yuan Shih-kai, China was breaking into independent fiefs controlled by warlords with private armies. Fighting was going on constantly between one group or another. Yet Mao took little interest in the skirmishes occuring in his own country. It was as if he was shunning the small-timers and going to the masters for instruction—instruction that came in very handy later when he commanded troops. It is significant that once when the army wanted to commandeer the school for a barracks, Mao organized his fellow student to repulse them. After the crisis was over, he said proudly, "I've commanded my first troops!"

According to Robert Payne, Mao was especially thrilled by the way the French commandeered taxicabs to rush troops to the front in 1914 to prevent the invading German army from attacking Paris. After the Hsin Min Study Association was formed by Mao and Siao-Yu, Mao would hold sessions in which he explained the European military tactics to his fellow members.

Siao-Yu claimed forty-five years later that the Hsin Min was the embryo of the Chinese Communist Party. He said that because so many Hsin Min members became high officials in the party in later years. However, the organization was not originally political at all. It was a fellowship group of young students who thought themselves superior to the rest. Their name, Hsin Min, translates as "New People." Eventually there were about 100 members, but the charter members numbered only eleven. "In the ardor of our youth, we considered ourselves eleven 'sages'—guardians of the wisdom of the ages!" Siao-Yu said later.

New members had to have the hundred percent vote of all

the other members. They were selected for their intellectual attainments and congeniality with those already in the society. Three girls were admitted late in 1914. One of them, Tao Szu-yung, was described by Siao-Yu as "the kindest, gentlest person I have ever known." Whether Mao agreed with that description is not known, but as time went by he would find more and more excuses to be near her. At one time their associates thought they would eventually be married, but it was never to happen, as we shall see later in the story.

Mao and Siao-Yu met another attractive young woman, Yang Kai-hui, through her father, Yang Huai-chung, one of their teachers. Mao had a great reverance for Professor Yang, as did all of his students. Yang was about fifty years old. He had studied in Germany, Japan and England before taking his doctor of philosphy degree at the University of Edinburgh in Scotland. In addition to his European education, Dr. Yang was deeply versed in the Confucian classics. In time his moral qualities earned him the name of the "Confucius of Changsha." He did much to sweep away Mao's prejudice against the ancient Chinese sage.

Dr. Yang often spoke of Mao as one of the best students he ever taught. His praise of Mao's essays provided some of the proudest moments of Mao's academic life up to that point. At that time Mao began to neglect many of his classes in order to spend time in the library seeking knowledge in his own way. However, he never missed one of Dr. Yang's classes.

Yang often invited his star pupils to dinner. His daughter ate with them. However Dr. Yang did not believe in talk at the table, so none of the young men got to speak to her. Siao-Yu was hopelessly in love with her. Like Mao, he had been married at an early age by his parents, but unlike Mao he had accepted his responsibility.

The political situation in China continued to worsen. Yuan Shih-kai was trying to restore the Monarchy. Sun Yat-sen and his Kuomintang Party were trying to set up a rival republic in Canton, where Dr. Sun had considerable strength. At the same time, various warlords were carving out provincial empires for themselves, fighting each other and Yuan Shih-kai's central government.

Mao had heard of communism from Tsai Ho-shen, a fellow member of the Hsin Min Study Association. He had been interested but not particularly impressed, because Tsai expressed himself badly. Later another friend gave Mao a translation of *The Communist Manifesto* by Karl Marx and Friedrich Engels. That book, written in 1848, launched communism in Europe.

Certain parts of Marx's theories appealed strongly to Mao. Marx argued that the world progresses through class struggle. This struggle, he said, was between the *bourgeoisie*—whom Marx identified as those who control production—and the *proletariat*, whom he identified as the working class. He insisted that the working man did not receive the full value of his labor because the owners kept the profits and shared them with the capitalists who had invested in the companies. Marx went on to argue that a nation's wealth would gradually be gathered into the hands of a few capitalists until it reached a point where the working class would revolt and seize control of the government. The result would be a dictatorship of the proletariat. This in turn would lead to a classless society with everything commonly owned. In Marx's idealistic view, this would eventually produce a society where armies, police and even governments would be unnecessary.

Mao was rapidly developing what became the best analytical mind of his time. From the first he put his finger on a major weakness of communism as expounded by Marx—the dictatorship of the proletariat, defined as industrial urban workers.

Marx had no interest in the peasant class at all. His studies had convinced him that peasants make poor revolutionists. Mao, coming from the soil himself, distrusted the city industrial workers and believed devoutly in the farmers as the source of strength for a Chinese revolution.

While he liked the idea of a world revolution to destroy bosses, Mao was disturbed because Marx's prediction had been made in 1848, and it was now 1917. Sixty-nine years had passed, and from what Mao gathered in his reading, capitalism had grown stronger rather than weaker in those years. This fact did not necessarily make him reject Marx's ideas, but he had never been one to accept any idea blindly. After thorough analysis he arrived at his own independent opinion and position.

Unfortunately for Mao, he still lacked sufficient knowledge of economic conditions in Europe and the United States to answer his own questions. He knew nothing of antitrust laws and the growth of labor unions. They had collectively done much to stop the squeeze on the working class which Marx had observed in Germany and England.

Lack of full understanding kept Mao from accepting communism at that time. However, the idea intrigued him. He wanted to know more about it but had difficulty finding information. He could not read any foreign language and no other books were available in Chinese translations. For some reason, he distrusted anything anybody told him but accepted information if it was in a book. He found a Russian refugee who had been a disciple of Nicolai Lenin but was not very much impressed by what little he could learn from him.

Politically Mao was still unsettled. He liked the idea of socialism and was against the present Republic. He had cheered it in 1911 but became disillusioned in 1915 when Yuan Shih-kai dissolved the parliament and attempted to rule autocratically by decree. After Yuan died in 1916, his successor, Li Yuan-hung, restored the parliament to prevent a new revolution.

Student resentment of the central government was not appeased by the restoration of parliament. The law-making body was torn by internal political dissension and dominated by antirepublican forces. It was totally ineffective, resulting in a weak government that permitted more and more warlords to seize command in the provinces.

Still worse, Japan joined the Allies in World War I. After seizing all of Germany's islands in the central Pacific, she then presented China with demands for Germany's concessions there. In addition the Japanese demanded that China appoint Japanese advisors to the Chinese government.

The students' rage was comparable to that which swept China when Japan took Korea after the Sino-Japanese War. However, the domestic chaos prevented any one group from massing sufficient strength to mount a revolution against Li's central government.

In the Canton region, Sun Yat-sen seemed the best possibility to unite China, but Mao had lost all respect for the leader of the Kuomintang. His inquiring mind had not yet found what he sought. In fact he did not really know what he was seeking. He knew only that he could not tolerate conditions as they were. Although he tried to keep his feelings from his companions, he felt a growing certainty that in some mysterious way destiny had selected him for a major role in changing China.

Just as he had given Emi Siao a glimpse of his true feelings by the expression on his face when he returned the book, *Heroes of the Western World*, Mao let slip another glimpse of his true feelings to Emi's brother.

It happened during an argument Siao-Yu and Mao had about the motives of the Emperor Liu Pang, who founded the Han dynasty in 202 B.C. In the summer of 1917 Mao, who was still a student at the Normal school, and Siao-Yu, who had graduated and was a teacher himself, went on a begging hike through Hunan. They decided that they could find out more about life and the people by doing this than by just plain traveling.

One evening, as they rested after an all-day tramp, they got to discussing Liu Pang and his motives in making himself emperor. Siao-Yu was critical of the Han founder, and Mao vehemently defended Liu Pang. Liu Pang had risen from a lowly beginning to become emperor. Siao-Yu said later that he broke off the argument, "lest I might criticize him [Mao] directly. We both knew he was identifying himself with Liu Pang."

This was not to Mao's discredit. It shows that he felt the press of destiny even in his teens, and that his decisive role in changing a shattered nation into a world power was not pure chance. Mao made his own opportunities and fought his way up step by step because he had youthful ambition and believed in himself.

During the tramp through Hunan the two friends had their fortunes told by a girl at an inn. She told Mao that he was audacious and ambitious, and that he was capable of killing a hundred thousand people without sentiment. She added that if he lived to be fifty he would have great luck. After fifty, his luck would increase day by day.

How did the girl's prophecy compare with what really happened? Mao was certainly ambitious and audacious. As for being capable of killing a hundred thousand without sentiment, in his battles, in the liquidation following the victorious civil war, and in forcing collectivism on the Chinese peasant, Mao was responsible for the deaths of far more than a hundred thousand. There is no evidence that he ever regretted it. He reached the age of 50 in 1943. His Red Army was then developing the strength that brought eventual victory, so we can say the prediction of good luck came true. And his fortunes did improve almost day by day after that, ending in triumph in 1949. All in all, it was a remarkably good prophecy.

The young men had intended to tramp all summer, but summer thaws jammed the Yangtze, sending flood waters splashing over their route, so they abandoned their jaunt and took a boat back to Changsha.

Mao went back to Changsha Normal to spend the rest of the summer, while Siao-Yu returned to his teaching. The two continued to meet in the evenings at gatherings of their Hsin Min group. Mao was developing considerable leadership ability, and his speaking style was also improving. An early acquaintance said he was a "charismatic" speaker and seemed at times divinely inspired.

The Hsin Min group got a dramatic new subject to talk about in mid-1917. China declared war on Germany. No one expected her to send troops to fight with the Allies in Europe. The declaration of war was a sly political move on the part of Li Yuan-hung to counter Japanese attempts to grab German land holdings and concessions in China. As one of the belligerents, China would have a place at the peace conference when the war ended. Since the United States had already entered the war against Germany, Li knew this would soon lead to Germany's defeat.

The Hsin Mins argued about whether Li was right or wrong. Mao sympathized with Li's motives but felt that the big powers would ignore weak China and her needs. Soon, however, their attention was electrified by the Russian Revolution. The revolt in Russia began in March, 1917, with the overthrow of the czar and the establishment of a provisional government. Mao had not been interested, for he felt that like China's revolution it was the exchange of one poor government for another. But when Communist forces overthrew the Kerensky provisional government in October, Mao followed events carefully, for the Communist leader, Lenin, was a Marxist. Mao was still very much interested in Marxism and had several times reread *The Communist Manifesto.*

The rest of the Hsin Min Study Association were electrified by the Communist victory. Many of them had already been converted to Marxism by their fellow member Tsai Ho-chen, whom Siao-Yu called "the first Chinese Communist." Mao seems to have been inspired by the way the Bolshevik Communists were able to seize power despite their small number, rather than by the triumph of the Communist ideology, as the others were. The Russian Communist Party had only 100,000 members but had been able to take over a nation of 160,000,000.

It was that practical side of revolution that Mao wanted to learn more about. It showed him that large masses of soldiers and supporters were not necessary to overthrow a government if the people would not support it. The Russian masses had not been pro-Communist, but they had been antigovernment. Consequently they did not fight to support Kerensky, nor did they oppose the Communist takeover.

As his interest grew in the practical, military side of the Russian revolution, Mao learned more about Marxism. The Russian Bolsheviks under Lenin thought that their victory would spark a worldwide revolt in other capitalistic countries, as Karl Marx had predicted. When it did not, they moved to "export" Communism. This brought an increased flow of translated Communist literature into China, along with a number of Communist teachers.

These sources of information were mostly to be found in Peking, Shanghai and Canton. Only a trickle of news got down to Changsha, but it was enough to show Mao that Russian Communism did not agree entirely with what he had read in *The Communist Manifesto.*

Mao now realized that he had to broaden himself by moving from Changsha to a larger city where he could get in contact with true revolutionists. The young men in the Hsin Min group were nothing but naive amateurs. Mao was by that time in his sixth year at the Changsha Normal school, but he had long since ceased to take the college itself seriously. He still attended a few lectures that appealed to him but spent most of his time in the library, reading from opening to closing time.

His chance to leave came suddenly in 1918. Two things happened to make it possible. One was that soon after China entered the war on the side of the Allies in 1917, Lloyd George of England suggested that China permit young people to go to France as work forces to take the places of Frenchmen who had been killed or taken into the army. The Chinese government was willing, and nearly 100,000 laborer-class coolies went to France. The other thing that worked to move

Mao to Peking was his friend Siao-Yu's burning desire to study in Europe.

Siao-Yu worked out a plan whereby members of the Hsin Min would be helped by the Franco-Chinese Educational Association to go to France as part-time workers and part-time students. He wrote his and Mao's old professor, Yang Huai-chung, who had moved to Peking University as a lecturer the previous year. Yang got in touch with Tsai Yuan-pei, head of the Franco-Chinese Educational Association. He wrote the Hsin Min that a student-worker program was already in operation and promised to work them into it.

Mao, Siao-Yu and eight others left immediately for Peking. All were excited at the prospect of going to France except Mao. His roots were sunk deep in Chinese soil, and he had no desire to pull them up.

His companions were dismayed. Mao had become their acknowledged leader. They could not understand his attitude. In the arguments that followed, he gave several reasons for it: He had failed miserably in all his foreign language studies in the university. He feared that a trip to France would be a repetition of his failure in the soapmaking school. Also, he felt that their Hsin Min Association needed someone to keep contact between it and its members in France.

Even more important to him, although he did not express this to his companions, were Mao's plans for greatly expanding the Hsin Min membership. He had now secretly set himself a membership goal of 100,000, the number of Communist Party members who had successfully launched the October Revolution in Russia.

Mao Tse-tung was then twenty-five years old. Nine years had passed since he had walked out of his home with his bundle of clothes on one end of a carry-pole and his copies of *All Men Are Brothers* and *The Romance of the Three Kingdoms* on the other. They had been nine years of aimlessly wandering, mentally and physically. Now at last he had formed in his mind a path that he intended to follow for the rest of his life. His experience in organizing the Hsin Min had shown him that he had the ability to lead men and to influence their thoughts. And the Communist success in Russia had shown him a way to channel those abilities into something concrete. A trip to France was a pleasant side road, but he felt that it would carry him away from the main road he was now resolved to travel.

4
The Conspirators

Although the eager students, accompanied by Mao Tse-tung, rushed off to Peking on the first lap of their trip, they had to wait several months before a place could be found for them in France. Even then, they would have to pay their own way, but the fare aboard a French merchant ship was only one-third the usual rate. Arrangements were made with the Franco-Chinese Association in Paris to care for them until they could find work.

For a short time after their arrival in Peking, they lived with Professor Yang, but then they moved to a two-room slum apartment. Winter comes early and is cold in Peking. Seven students slept together in the only bed. Fortunately however, it was larger than the average bed. It was what is called a *kang*, a kind of bed that is used in Manchuria. Actually it is a long flat brick stove, with bedding piled on top and a low fire built in the firebox. The warmed bricks keep away the chill of the frigid Manchurian nights.

The kang works well if the fire is kept low enough to avoid scorching the sleepers. There was no danger of that, however, for the students from Changsha. They had no fuel at all and had to huddle together in the bed for mutual warmth. Years later Mao told Edgar Snow that they were packed so closely that he had to warn his companions when he wanted to turn over in bed.

Siao-Yu was the first to leave. Dr. Li had chosen him to be secretary of the Franco-Chinese Association, and he left in November, 1918, for Paris. The others—all except Mao—followed in the early part of 1919.

Mao Tse-tung was penniless. Tsai Yuan-pei arranged with the chief librarian at the Peking University, Li Ta-chao, for Mao to take a job as library helper. (Li Ta-Chao is not to be confused with the Dr. Li who arranged the Paris trips.)

Mao's decision to take the menial position in the library was a fateful one. Unknown to him, Li Ta-chao, in collaboration with Chen Tu-hsiu, the Dean of Literature at the university, was already in contact with Russian agents in regard to forming a Communist Party in China. Several months before, Li Ta-chao had written a complimentary article about the Russian October Revolution. Lenin, deeply interested in exporting Communism, immediately sent agents to talk secretly with the author. Li Ta-chao discussed the offer with Chen Tu-hsiu, who also sympathized with the Russian Revolution. They decided that it was too risky to sponsor an official Communist Party at that time. Instead, they decided to put their efforts into a Marxist Study Association at the university.

The announced purpose of the Marxist Study Association was to investigate the principles of Marxism from a purely scholarly viewpoint. In actuality, the purpose was to gather recruits and to find out which the professors could trust to form a Communist Party later. While Siao-Yu claimed that the Hsin Min Study Association he and Mao founded was the embryo of the future Communist Party because half its members became Communists, the real father of the Party in China was Li Ta-chao.

Mao Tse-tung, busily trying to figure out how he could turn Communism to his own ambitious purposes, was not aware of all this. He did know that there were a number of radicals and Communist sympathizers in the university. He hoped that his work in the library would bring him into contact with them. Radicals and would-be revolutionists had to be cautious. They would not talk to a stranger.

There was also an element of snobbishness in their refusal to talk to Mao. He was employed as a sweeper and was the clerk who brought them newspapers. As a result, Mao's hope of enlisting many of them into his Hsin Min Study Association did not materialize. Mao grew moody and was disappointed in the university. He had pinned much hope on finding congenial souls there. After the second and last group of his friends left for France, Mao quit the university job and began another tramp through the country. Strangely enough, one of the places he visited was the birthplace of Confucius, whom he had hated so much as a child.

Mao's wandering took him back to Changsha in 1919. It was not homesickness that drew him back to his native province. Hunan was under the control of a warlord named Chang Ching-yao, whose tyranny and viciousness were stirring the hot-tempered Hunanese into a new revolt. Mao hoped to take advantage of the trouble. One of the plotters against Chang was Professor Yi Pei-chi, who had been one of Mao's teachers at the First Normal. Professor Yi gladly accepted Mao's offer to help. He put his former student to work as an agitator to arouse the students. It was a task for which Mao was ideally fitted. His clear logic and burning enthusiasm for violent action against the warlord brought a flood of recruits to Professor Yi.

He founded a Hsin Min newspaper whose inflammatory style made it a great hit with Changsha students. After a few issues it was suppressed by Governor Chang Ching-yao. Mao found it expedient to return to Peking for a while to escape the governor's police. This time his reception at the university was different from what it had been when he was only a library porter. Professor Yi had been impressed by Mao's organizational ability and gave him a splendid recommendation to Chen Tu-hsiu, who was plotting a student uprising to coincide with the coming May 4 anniversary of Japan's first demands on China.

Chen took time from his busy schedule to advise Mao how to conduct his struggle against the warlord of Hunan. Then he introduced Mao to Li Ta-chao. Although Li had provided Mao with the university library job earlier, he had never met Mao. He had received Tsai's request to give Mao a job and had passed it along to a subordinate to carry out. After listening to the young agitator from Changsha, both Li and Chen were greatly impressed. Li told Chen that Mao would be very valuable to them when the time came to form the Chinese Communist Party.

Shortly after that, a former governor of Hunan led a successful revolt that overthrew warlord Chang. Professor Yi had been one of the new governor's supporters and was rewarded with a high state position in the new provincial government. Yi immediately sent for Mao, rewarding the young man's hard work by appointing him director of the Primary School Section at Changsha Normal. Mao then used his official position in the school to build up the membership of his Hsin Min Study Association. This was done with Professor Yi's full approval.

Mao now had very definite plans for the society he and Siao-Yu had formed. To the consternation of the co-founder in Paris, Mao began changing the Association into a Communist Front organization.

Up to that time Mao had dedicated himself to his work. Now he had really fallen in love. The first girl his name was associated with was Tao Szu-yung, one of the three girl-students who had joined the Hsin Min Study Association at its founding six years before. She and Mao were very close for a while and in the early part of 1920 they jointly operated a liberal book store in Changsha. They broke up in the middle part of the year. One story said their estrangement came over Mao's Communistic leanings.

Siao-Yu said, "They were deeply in love, but because they held different political ideas, she finally left him and founded a school, Li Ta Hsueh Yuan, in Shanghai. She died in that city about 1930."

However, Szu-yung certainly had known of Mao's growing interest in Communism a long time before they parted. Mao was forever explaining the principles of Marxism at Hsin Min meetings years before this. Also the "Library of Culture" they formed in Changsha in early 1920 was designed solely to distribute Marxist propaganda. It seems more likely that Mao, having again seen Yuan Kai-hui during his visit to Peking, found that he had never forgotten the pretty daughter of his old professor.

In any event, Tao Szu-yang left about June, and within a few weeks Mao married Yang Kai-hui. Both Emi Siao and Siao-Yu have left records attesting to her gentleness and education. In his "Autobiography," originally published in Peking from a translation taken from Edgar Snow's *Red Star Over China*, Mao gives only one sentence to his marriage: "In the same year (1920) I married Yang Kai-hui." In a footnote to this sentence, Snow added, "She was from all accounts a brilliant woman, a student of Peking National University, later a leader of youth during the Great Revolution, and one of the most active women Communists . . . and they were evidently very devoted."

In later years Yang Kai-hui was arrested by Nationalist police and executed. Snow places the time as 1930. Siao-Yu said it was 1927, and that she was killed simply because she was the wife of Mao Tse-tung. This ignores the fact that Yang Kai-hui herself was a very efficient and brilliant Communist Youth organizer. Siao-Yu, then a professor in Nanking and a Kuomintang official, tried to save her but was unable to do so. As a result, in his book, *Mao Tse-tung and I Were Beggars*, Siao-Yu has some bitter things to say about Mao.

While he does not pretend to speak for Yang Kai-hui's feelings in the matter, Siao-Yu claims that he himself was her father's choice for her husband, but that his own early marriage prevented this. Then Siao-Yu quotes a mutual friend who said, "The one who killed Yang Kai-hui was Jun-chih." Jun-chih was Mao's student name.

As for his own thoughts in the matter, Siao-Yu wrote a bitter poem about the impossibility of his love for Yang Kai-hui, ending it with these lines:

> Another had no heart. He abandoned his wife for the sake of ambition.
> His wife hates him in another world.

The living can hardly speak for the dead, and no one really knows what Yang Kai-hui thought when the executioner's bullets ripped into her brain, but the living can speak for themselves. Mao, after long years of silence about his first wife of his own choosing, let down the curtain about his heart for one brief glimpse. This happened after the final Communist victory, when Mao Tse-tung had become a national hero and the ruler of Red China.

A woman who lost her beloved husband in the revolution had written a sad poem in memory of her loss. She sent the poem to Mao. He replied with a poem of his own in which he said, "I lost my proud poplar and you your willow . . . ." The name of the woman's husband translates as "willow" and Yang means "poplar." Mao's verse goes on to describe the vision in his mind's eye of their departed spouses' tears in heaven—tears of joy as they look down to see the success of the revolution for which they gave their lives.

All this, of course, was far in the future at the time Mao Tse-tung brought his bride home to Changsha. They lived first in a house at the edge of the city, near a large lake. There were five rooms enclosed in a small courtyard that was planted as a garden. The floors were dirt. A Japanese newspaperman, visiting the house recently, reported that the bedroom had a large rosewood bed that occupied half the floor space. Presumably the bed, which had lattices covered with paintings of birds and flowers on silk, had been a wedding present from Professor Yang to his beloved daughter and her new husband.

One of the rooms was a spare bedroom where Mao put up various comrades who were passing through Changsha. The living room was the Hunan headquarters for what became the provincial Communist Party. Mao now saw his goal clearly and worked feverishly to build up a Marxist group that he intended to have as his weapon in the power struggle that lay ahead.

This was a comparatively quiet and easy period of Mao's life, although he worked hard. His official position with the government ended when Governor Tan was displaced by a new warlord, Chao Heng-ti. Chao began his militarist regime with protestations of democracy, but as he became more solidly entrenched, his policies changed.

Probably because of the influence of Li Ta-chao and Chen Tu-hsiu, Mao had taken an antimilitarist position. He pursued a course of organizing students, workers and citizens into strike and protest groups, disdaining formal army fighting. In one notable attack, he led shouting students in an assault on the provincial parliament building. They broke through the guards and ripped down scrolls and propaganda hangings put up by the military government. Members of the parliament, all of whom were landed gentry appointed by the new warlord, fled.

Another time he organized a public demonstration to celebrate the anniversary of the Russian October Revolution. That was suppressed by the police, as was a parade he tried to stage to demonstrate for equal rights for women.

These suppressions and the tight clamp that the provincial police kept on his activities slowly changed Mao's ideas. He came around to the idea that civil disobedience activities would never be successful and that armed military revolution was the only way he could hope to succeed in bringing a Marxist government to China.

While Mao Tse-tung was learning the art of organization and leading men in Hunan, the Hunanese students in France were organizing a Chinese Communist Party there. Another group of Chinese students in Germany were likewise organizing a Communist group. Names later to become famous in Communist history, Chou En-lai, Li Li-san, and Chu Teh, were among them. Chou En-lai, born of a wealthy family, in time became the Chinese Communist best known to the Western world. Li Li-san, burly, loud-mouthed and aggressively sure of himself, would eventually plot the course of Communism's fight in China. And Chu Teh, ex-Nationalist general, ex-opium smoker, ex-police chief, was to become the greatest general in modern Chinese history. At that time, however, they, like Mao Tse-tung, were seeking to find themselves.

Late in 1920, Siao-Yu, who took no part in the Communist activities of the Chinese student-workers in France, returned to China on Franco-Chinese Educational Association business. He was not able to get in touch with Mao until the spring of 1921. He was dismayed to find then that Mao had no more interest in their Hsin Min society but had turned totally into a Marxist. They had long arguments in which Mao tried to convince his old friend to follow him down the Marxist trail.

When Siao-Yu argued that the necessary changes would come in time through less totalitarian methods than those the Communists employed, Mao said impatiently: "I admire your patience in being willing to wait a hundred or a thousand years. I cannot wait even ten years. I want us to achieve our aims tomorrow!"

Their friendship had now reached the crossroads. Both knew it, but Mao, who had a genuine affection for his old friend, tried to patch up the disagreement. He told Siao-Yu that he was going to Shanghai to attend a meeting to form the official Chinese Communist Party at last. He insisted that his friend go with him.

Siao-Yu refused. Mao insisted, promising to introduce his friend to top Chinese Marxists as well as the representative of the Comintern (Communist International) who was expected to be present. Siao-Yu agreed to accompany Mao to Shanghai but refused to attend the meeting, which was held in July, 1921. The Comintern had been organized by Lenin to direct Communist revolts around the world. The Comintern representative was a Dutch Communist known as Maring, whose real name was Hendricus Sneevliet. The meeting was arranged by Chen Tu-hsiu and Li Ta-chao.

Maring arrived late, missing the first part of the meeting, so the initial group were nine Chinese, including Mao Tse-tung, who represented the Hunan Communists. The conspirators' meeting place was a girls' school in the French concession area of Shanghai. The school was closed for the summer season, and Chen and Li arranged through their friends, the school authorities, to make use of it. The school's cook had remained for the summer as a night watchman. He had orders to admit the nine Communists and to prepare food for them.

According to Chen Pan-tsu, one of the members who wrote an account in the *Communist International* magazine fifteen years later, the delegates were to define the basic tasks of the new Party in line with current political situations, to develop Party laws, and build an organization.

They immediately broke into an argument over which direction the new Party should take. Chen claimed Li Han-chun's argument was that the Chinese proletariat lacked sufficient political training to back a revolution. He wanted to work through an enlightened middle class to educate the working class before moving into the mainstream of Marxism.

Another delegate, Liu Jen-ching, was adamant in demanding that the party immediately back a proletariat dictatorship along strict Marxist lines. Mao Tse-tung disagreed with both and spoke for an agrarian policy founded on the peasant class. His suggestion was rudely brushed aside by the others. Their final decision was a compromise between the two extremes offered. The party platform called for organizing the proletariat but working with the bourgeoisie, at least in the beginning. They adopted the policy of working through the trade unions and called for an organization based upon that of the Bolshevik Russians.

On the fourth day of the conference the conspirators met in the apartment of Li Han-tsin, the moderate, before going on to the Girls' School. Soon after they arrived, at 8 P.M., a suspicious character in a long coat was observed at the door. Li Han-tsin went to question him. The man said suavely that he was seeking the chairman of the Association of Social Organizations, a man who lived three houses away. The stranger apologized and departed quickly.

Li Han-tsin quickly alerted his co-conspirators. The Association of Social Organizations was a legitimate office, but it had no chairman. It operated under an executive secretary. The spy—for they were now sure he was one—had made a slip through ignorance. The conspirators hastily grabbed their documents and slipped out the back door to fade into the dark night. Mao circled back to watch the house.

Within ten minutes he saw the police arrive. They searched the apartment but could find nothing upon which to base an arrest of Li Han-tsin, who had stayed at the apartment. If he had fled also, it would have been proof to the police that there had been an illegal meeting.

The others were afraid to return to the Girls' School, for they suspected now that it was under surveillance; otherwise they did not see how they had been traced to Li Han-tsin's apartment. They had to find other places to sleep that night. Mao returned to stay with Siao-Yu, who had accompanied Mao to Shanghai, although he had refused to attend the Communist Party organization meeting.

The organization had not been completed. The delegates decided that it was not safe to confer for the entire seven days that they had originally scheduled, but they felt that one more day's planning was imperative. They first selected a vacation spot near Chiahsing in Chekiang province, about a hundred miles from Shanghai. Mao and Siao-Yu rode down on the train, which was jammed with vacationers.

Again Siao-Yu refused to attend the Communist meeting. He waited at the hotel until it was over. The plan called for the conspirators to rent a boat like the vacationers and to do their plotting on the lake well out of hearing of any spy. They chose a sampan with an arched mat covering. It was well that they did, for it was a gray day and misty rain began to fall before they finished their meeting. This in itself was fortunate for them, for it cut down the number of vacationers who chose to go boating. They had the lake pretty much to themselves. They carried picnic lunches and wine in bottles to add to their cover as a group on a holiday.

Maring arrived in time for this final meeting. He played only a small part in the discussions, but that part was to affect the Party for the next twenty-two years. Opposition to his policy in time caused Mao Tse-tung's demotion in the Central Party Committee and affected Russian-Chinese relations down to this very day.

According to organizer Chen Tan-chiu, the discussions went on all day and did not end until eleven o'clock that night. They readily agreed on the outstanding organizational policies and rules for Party discipline, but they almost broke apart over Maring's demand that the Communist Party members become members of Dr. Sun Yat-sen's Kuomintang Parry and work within Sun's group.

This resulted in a violent argument. Part of the group complained that Dr. Sun's Kuomintang Party was allied to the money class. However, Maring was adamant. Lenin had known Sun Yat-sen when both were plotting revolution. They had discussed the revolutionary futures of both their countries while in exile in London. Lenin was convinced that Sun Yat-sen was a true Marxist and that any intimation he gave otherwise was a sham to deceive Western nations. Chen

Tan-chiu claimed later that Maring gave them an ultimatum: They had to cooperate with Sun Yat-sen or Russia would withdraw support.

Harold Isaacs talked with Maring in later years, and Maring denied Chen's claim. Maring told Isaacs that he did not insist on Communist-Kuomintang cooperation. He said he suggested it and the others readily agreed.

After this agreement the meeting broke up. Mao returned to the hotel room where Siao-Yu waited for him. For a long time they lay awake in bed arguing about the merits of Communism. Mao was unable to convince his friend. Although they corresponded for several years after that, their long friendship was breaking up. Within a few weeks Mao led the Marxist sympathizers out of the Hsin Min Study Association, making them the nucleus of the Communist Party in Hunan.

As a result of the decision made on the boating party, a number of Communist Party members also joined the Kuomintang, but it was not until 1923, at the third Congress of the Communist Party, that delegates agreed to join the Kuomintang in a united front to drive the warlords out of North China and unite the country.

The years between were busy ones for Mao Tse-tung. He was rapidly developing his own program, which was often at odds both with the Kuomintang Party of Dr. Sun Yat-sen and with the Chinese Communist Party of Chen Tu-hsiu. Mao showed very early that he did not intend to be either a mere cog in the Red machine or a blind follower.

His stubborn attitude and confident belief in his own policies put him on a direct collision course with his superiors in the Party.

5

The Independent Communist

China in the 1920s was a land of almost total political chaos. The country had not known a day of peace since the beginning of the revolution in 1911. One warlord after another took command in Peking, while provincial warlords carved out their own individual kingdoms throughout the country. In Canton Dr. Sun Yat-sen was trying to fight the southern warlords while he built the foundation of another republic. The Chinese Communist Party, in obedience to Moscow's orders, tried to work with Dr. Sun. Mao Tse-tung, an individualist always, took his own road.

After the Communist Party was formed in 1921, Mao went to Hunan to set up trade unions and organize strikes. It was the Party policy to concentrate on the working classes. Mao did his part but disagreed with the emphasis put on city workers to the exclusion of the peasant classes. However, his organizing pleased Chen Tu-hsiu, who now headed the Party.

The fastest-rising star among the young Communists was

not Mao. It was Li Li-san, who had been one of those who formed the French branch of the Chinese Communist Party in Paris before returning to China. Siao-Yu described him as a boor and a loud-mouth who had overconfidence in his own ability and intellect.

Once Li Li-san interrupted a Paris meeting by shouting: "Li Li-san road!" This meant they should follow his guidance. Eventually the Party did chose to follow the "Li Li-san road," and it almost destroyed them all. Li Li-san had an urban background himself. This made him ardently in favor of the Russian Comintern policy of depending upon the urban workers as the base for building their power.

In Hunan, Mao was deeply involved in the riots that followed the execution of two young anarchists by Hunan's governor, Chao Heng-ti. Mao was not an anarchist. Anarchists are against any kind of government. Mao insisted, "If leaders have no power, it is impossible to carry out our plans. The more power a leader has, the easier it is to get things done." However, as secretary of the Communist Party in Hunan, he cooperated closely with the anarchists. He justified this action to Edgar Snow by saying: "We compromised with them and through negotiations prevented many hasty and useless actions by them."

From another source it appears that Mao was working to prevent the anarchists from committing violence simply for violence's sake. He attempted to guide their defiance against specific targets in a way that benefited the growing Communist Party in China.

Sun Yat-sen had not taken kindly to the original Russian demand for cooperation between the Chinese Communist Party and his own Kuomintang Party. However, after an attempt to get United States aid failed, he realized that he had to have Russian support. The Communists proved of great assistance to him, and by late 1924 Sun Yat-sen's grasp on the Canton region was sufficiently strong for him to consider mounting an attack on the northern warlords.

At that time Chang Tso-lin, warlord of Manchuria, attacked

Peking. Sun gave him aid under the mistaken belief that Chang would help Sun unite China under the Kuomintang rule. When this did not materialize as Sun hoped, he made plans to go to Peking to confer with Chang Tso-lin, known as the "Old Marshal." Dr. Sun died of cancer of the liver before he could put his plan into action. Leadership of the Kuomintang Party then passed in 1925 to Wang Ching-wei, who made a young soldier named Chiang Kai-shek commander-in-chief of the Kuomintang army. That appointment started Chiang on a rise that was swift and bloody, eventually bringing him and Mao Tse-tung together in a personal struggle that was to continue for the rest of their lives.

Chiang Kai-shek came from a well-to-do merchant family in Chekiang. He had been in a military school in Peking when Dr. Sun launched the Chinese Revolution in 1911. Chiang immediately joined the revolutionary army. The fighting ended quickly, but he succeeded in making some powerful friends among the senior officers.

When the fighting stopped, he left the army and started a stock brokerage business. After it collapsed, Chiang rejoined the army at the invitation of Sun Yat-sen, who sent him to Russia in 1923 to study the organization of the Red Army. Chiang returned to Canton in 1924 to start the Whampoa Military Academy for Sun Yat-sen. Whampoa is an island in the Pearl River off Canton. In earlier years it had been the port for foreign tea clippers.

Chiang did a remarkable job in running the academy, although he was aided by Mikhail Borodin and other Russian advisors. Borodin came from Moscow as personal advisor to Sun Yat-sen. Some of the best officers in the Kuomintang and Communist armies were Whampoa graduates.

When Sun Yat-sen died, there were naturally several candidates for his position. Three were murdered, permitting Wang Ching-wei to take over command of the party. Chiang Kai-shek's assumption of the army command seems to have been through pressure exerted on Wang by Borodin.

Stalin, the future Russian tyrant, was then engaged in a bitter power struggle with Leon Trotsky. Stalin was extremely interested in a friendly China. When Borodin assured him that their best bet in China was Chiang, Stalin ordered the Comintern to back Chiang Kai-shek in every possible way.

It is difficult to plot the devious course of politics and events in China at that time. "Authorities" give different views, depending upon their political sympathies and the narrowness of their sources. Benjamin I. Schwartz's book *Chinese Communism and the Rise of Mao*, gives what seems to be a more honest appraisal of the time than anyone else. He wrote: "The period of the Kuomintang-Communist collaboration (1923-1927) is, without doubt, one of the most confusing and complex periods in modern history. Almost all the sources, and the Communist sources in particular, are open to grave suspicion."

Since this is the story of Mao Tse-tung and not that of the Communist Party, the events and tangled scheming of those years are not our concern here except as they involved Mao himself. As for Mao, the period is an obscure one in his life, with many blanks and mysteries for the biographer. He was at odds with the Communist Party in 1923. Two different and opposing sources claim that Mao was expelled from his top party position that year. No reason is given. Probably it was because he pursued his own course instead of following the Party line, which is what caused his later expulsions.

All Mao has to say about it in his *Autobiography* as related to Edgar Snow is that he left Hunan after the big general strike in May and went to Shanghai, where he worked in the executive bureau of the Kuomintang Party. Apparently he had been stripped of his title of Secretary of the Communist Party in Hunan. This brought him into contact with Wang Ching-wei, who would succeed Sun Yat-sen, but apparently Mao made little impression on Wang.

Mao worked there, coordinating affairs between the Communist Party and the Kuomintang Party, until the winter of 1924, when he became seriously ill and returned to Hunan to recuperate. His arch rival, Li Li-san, who had done so well organizing the miners of Hunan, went to Russia at the same time. One report claims that Mao went back to Shao-Shan, but this is hard to substantiate. It probably derives from his report that he went home. By that time Mao had nothing to tie him to Shao-Shan. His mother was dead. His sister had married and his two brothers had joined the Communist movement. He now called Changsha home, and it was there that he and Yang Kai-hui went so he could recuperate.

That at least was his excuse for returning to Hunan. He may not have needed recuperation as much as he claimed, for in a short time he was again embroiled in a strenuous campaign to organize peasant unions to strike against their landlords. Mao had been unhappy in his desk job in Shanghai and probably exaggerated his ailment to get away. In any event he was so successful in his peasant organization that Chao Heng-ti, the Hunan governor, sent troops to wipe Mao out. It is significant that when Mao fled, he did not go back to Shanghai but made his way to Canton.

In Canton Mao worked for the Kuomintang. For a time he was secretary to Hu Han-min. Then Hu left hurriedly for Moscow after being implicated in the political assassinations that permitted Wang Ching-wei and Chiang Kai-shek to achieve control of the Kuomintang Party. After that, Mao became one of Wang's secretaries and an important figure in the Kuomintang Propaganda Department. His progress was rapid and he was proposed for membership in the Kuomintang's Central Committee.

Apparently Mao's specific duty was to further the cause of the Left Wing of the Kuomintang Party. Much of his writing for the paper put out by the Propaganda Department was devoted to attacking Tai Chio-Tao, who headed the Party's Right Wing.

Mao now became completely rabid on the subject of building a peasant resistance army. Before, he had been deeply interested in the possibility and thought the Communist Party should use the tremendous revolutionary potential of the mass of farmers, but he had never pushed the idea very hard.

However, his work in organizing the peasant unions prior to coming to Canton had given him an insight into the farmers' feelings and strengthened his conviction that the Communist Party should abandon the industrial proletariat as a revolutionary base and concentrate completely on the peasants. Mao put his ideas into an article called *"An Analysis of the Different Classes of Chinese Society."* He argued that the Chinese farmer, if properly led, could become a vital revolutionary force. He also argued for radical land reform and vigorous organization among the peasants.

Chen Tu-hsiu took violent exception to the article and refused to permit it to be published in any of the Communist Party organs. Mao was no more inclined to abide by Chen's dictatorial manners than he had been to knuckle down to Mao Jen-sheng's tyranny. He arranged for its publication in two of the Kuomintang papers that had come under his jurisdiction when he was head of the propaganda department. One was the *Peasant Monthly* and the other was *Chinese Youth*.

At this critical period in his life, it was very clear to Mao Tse-tung that his ideas were at such odds with those of the ruling clique of both the Communist and Kuomintang parties that he could not ever expect to dominate either. It was characteristic of his rebel soul that he refused to abandon his personal policies. He had never been one to act impulsively. Every decision he made was as carefully thought out as his classical school essays had been. He never made a decisive move without the most thorough analysis. But once he made a basic strategic decision, it was extremely difficult to change his mind.

The Chinese Communist Party's Russian-dominated hierarchy insisted—following Karl Marx's lead—that they had to work through the proletariat. In highly industrialized Europe, Marx had been on sure ground with such assumptions. His research had shown that the peasants had played a very poor part in every European revolt. They would fight with unrivaled ferocity when taxed beyond limits of endurance or when their land and homes were threatened, but once the particular personal threat was lifted, they went back to tilling their soil. They did not care one way or the other who ruled or what political philosophy governed as long as they could till their soil without burdensome taxes.

The situation was different in China. There ninety percent of the peasants were tenants who had to give as much as seventy percent of their crops to absentee landlords. Mao believed that land reform would draw the farmers into the Communist orbit and give them a goal to fight for.

Mao did not base his ideas on theory. While organizing unions in Hunan, he had hiked across the hills and valleys, visiting hundreds of farms and villages, talking, arguing, and explaining what Communism had to offer the Chinese peasants.

As a peasant himself, Mao Tse-tung had carried manure until his shoulders ached under the burden of his carry pole. He had waded through sucking mud or rice paddies to plow and plant seedlings. He had chased the paddy birds and fought locusts who tried to devour his father's growing crops. And he had swung a scythe until he nearly dropped with fatigue.

He had never gone hungry, for Mao Jen-sheng had sufficient to feed his family adequately if not liberally. However, Mao had seen hundreds of tenant farmers starving every winter after most of their crops had been seized for taxes and shares for rapacious landowners. He understood the Chinese peasant, his needs and his desires.

In inflaming the peasants, Mao in effect was declaring war on Stalin of Russia, Chen of the Chinese Communist Party, and Chiang Kai-shek of the Kuomintang. It took an unusual boldness to oppose such powerful leaders. But it was characteristic of Mao that he was willing to fight anybody and everybody once his goal was established.

Each of these leaders had definite reasons for opposing

Mao's passion for leading an agrarian revolution. Chiang Kai-shek was pushing for Russian assistance in leading an army against the northern warlords. He did not want peasant uprisings to interfer with his projected campaign. He seems to have been contemptuous of guerrilla-type fighting, which would be all the peasants could do. Chiang, as the former head of the Whampoa Military Academy, put his faith in orthodox military tactics. Stalin, who was rapidly eliminating all opposition on his way to total dictatorship of Russia, also was contemptuous of the peasant military-revolutionary possibilities. Stalin believed that Chiang Kai-shek had the best chance to defeat the various provincial Chinese warlords and unify the country. As a result, he ordered the Comintern—and through them the Chinese Communist Party—to support Chiang Kai-shek to the limit.

Chiang, however, proved difficult to work with. He leaned heavily on the advice of Mikhail Borodin, but subsequent events proved that Chiang's rapport with the Russians was pure opportunism. He wanted Russian Support for his Northern Campaign, as he called his projected drive against Chang Tso-lin in Peking.

When Russia tried to discourage the Northern Campaign, Chiang suddenly pulled a *coup d'etat* in Canton. He seized control of the Kuomintang Party command and imprisoned his leading Communist and Russian advisors. This was in March 1926.

Harold Isaac's account of the coup reads: "Morning found Chiang Kai-shek master of Canton. It also found the other leaders of the Kuomintang in a state of panic and confusion . . . . They were all badly frightened."

The leftists in the Kuomintang Party looked to the Communist Party for support and got none. Stalin still considered Chiang Kaishek the best bet to unify China and thought Chiang's coup nothing more than a personal power grab. Since Stalin was trying to build up his own power in Russia, he did not feel that Chiang's actions were aimed directly at the

Communists. When no aid was forthcoming from either the Russians or the Chinese Communists, Wang Ching-wei hastily resigned as head of the Kuomintang Party, leaving Chiang in complete control.

The Kuomintang legalized Chiang's grip on the party by formally electing him chairman at a May 15 (1926) meeting. Chiang, in turn, issued drastic regulations to control Communists within the Party. Communists were banned from Party and Government top department posts, limited to one third of the membership of provincial organizations, and ordered to support the principles of the late Dr. Sun Yat-sen.

Borodin had been away during the coup. He either returned of his own accord or was sent back by Stalin. Stalin, caught unaware by Chiang's sudden action, ordered Borodin and the Comintern to cooperate with Chiang. Borodin, attempting to save his own face, claimed later that he advised Chiang to seize power. In any event, Borodin was able to patch up matters sufficiently to restore the coalition government of Kuomintang-Communist cooperation. However, the Communist portion was greatly restricted in its actions. Chiang then forced Borodin to back the Northern Campaign. The expedition began in July and within three months had swept through Hunan, Hupeh, Kiangsi, Anhwei and Kiangsu. By December, Chiang was in control all the way from Canton to the Yangtze River and was preparing to attack Shanghai.

The extraordinary progress of the victorious Nationalist Army was made possible by spontaneous uprisings of peasants and workers along its route. In Hunan, where Mao had worked so hard to organize peasant unions immediately before going to Canton, the Nationalist Army of Chiang Kai-shek had only to move in; the fighting was done for them before they arrived. Rebels took Changsha and delivered it to Chiang.

All this was a tribute to Mao Tse-tung, but Chiang Kai-shek was not at all pleased. He did not want uprisings of the workers, and he did not want support from the peasants. At that critical stage, considering the great support he was getting from both, this may seem strange. But Chiang was already plotting a future secret attack on the Communists and did not want strong Communist-led groups to face him.

As for the peasants, he well knew that their real reason for fighting was the hope of land reform. They wanted their landlords driven out and the land divided among themselves. This they had been promised by Mao Tse-tung, but a majority of the Kuomintang officers who supported Chiang Kai-shek were themselves landowners or the sons of landowners. Land reform to them was utter heresy.

The Communist Party continued to support—albeit, unwillingly—Chiang's policies. And Mao Tse-tung continued to work against both his own party and the Kuomintang. Mao left Canton soon after Chiang's coup and went to Shanghai. In the meantime, under Russian pressure, the Communists and the Kuomintang again tried to operate a coalition government. Its headquarters was established at Wuhan. Wuhan is not a city actually, but is a district or industrial complex made up of the three cities of Hanyang, Hankow and Wuchang on the Yangtze River in Hupeh Province.

Mao soon left Shanghai to make another trip through Hunan. He then sent a report to the Communist Party headquarters urging that the party take advantage of the tremendous revolutionary power of the peasant movement. The report was ignored. So in the spring of 1927 Mao went to Wuhan to present his ideas in person. They involved redistribution of land to poor farmers, and an interprovincial meeting of peasant union leaders had enthusiastically endorsed them. Despite this backing, Chen Tu-hsiu angrily refused to let Mao speak before the Central Committee.

While this was going on, Chiang Kai-shek was moving on Shanghai. By the middle of February, 1927, he was only fifty miles from the city. Inside the city, Chou En-lai and other Communist organizers were stirring up strikes to support Chiang. The city's bankers seemed curiously undisturbed by

Mao as a young peasant organizer in 1927. *China Pictorial Photo*.

Chiang's approach, even though he was supported by both Stalin of Russia and the Chinese Communists. The fateful significance of the bankers' indifference seems to have escaped the attention of Stalin, Borodin and Chen Tu-hsiu.

In late February, the Communist labor unions launched a devastating strike, and the military governor, Li Pao-chang, struck back with a reign of terror. Squads of soldiers roamed the streets executing suspected Communists where they found them. A dispatch to the New York *Herald Tribune* (quoted by Isaacs) reported:

"The executioners, bearing broad swords . . . forced the strikers to bend over while their heads were cut off. Thousands fled in terror while heads were stuck on sharp-pointed bamboo poles and were hoisted aloft and carried to the scene of the next execution."

The beleaguered strikers thought that Chiang Kai-shek, whose army was only fifty miles away, would march to their aid. Chiang gave an order to halt the advance. A claim was made later that this was done deliberately to permit Li Pao-chang to kill as many of the left-wing strikers as possible before Chiang took the city. Despite this clear indication of anti-Communist sentiment, Stalin still demanded that the Chinese Communist Party cooperate with Chiang.

The strike was broken but resumed again in March. British, Japanese and American troops were landed to protect the International Settlement in Shanghai. Chiang again delayed his march on Shanghai, although militarily there were no obstacles in his way.

That time, the Communist organizers planned more carefully. The attacks opened in six parts of the city and engulfed the total lower-class population. When the workers began winning, Chiang reversed his order and his Nationalist troops moved on Shanghai at last.

The Communist organizers, who expected to be praised for preparing the city for Chiang's triumph, got a shocking surprise. Chiang Kai-shek moved into Shanghai on March 26,

1927. The situation looked good for him to advance to Peking without serious difficulty, finally uniting China again. This was a crucial point for Chiang. He felt that he must now make a positive decision about his future course of action. He had gone that far with Communist support, but he was not himself a Communist despite his Russian schooling and his coalition government with the Chinese Communist Party. He now had to move either completely into the Communist camp or else completely to the right. In secret conferences the bankers of Shanghai promised him heavy loans to finance his drive on Peking, and they acted as go-betweens for bringing Chiang into rapport with the top leaders of the foreign settlement. Even before he took Shanghai, Chiang had already decided to align himself with the moneyed group. A little later he made the alliance personal by marrying Soong Mei-ling, sister of Mrs. Sun Yat-sen and a member of the financially powerful Soong family of bankers.

For years there had been a rumor that Chiang in his early days was connected with the "Green Gang," a secret society of criminals led by a police official in Shanghai. This story has never been proven. However, it is a fact that the Kuomintang used the Green Gang as its chief shock troops against the Communists when Chiang finally made his move against his former allies before dawn on April 12. A bugler atop Chiang's headquarters building gave the signal. Shock troops started to move out to attack the labor organizations and their people.

Hundreds were shot down in the streets. Hundreds more were captured and led away to execution. Among those captured were Ku Chen-chung, a leader of the General Labor Union, and his assistant, Chou En-lai. Both managed to escape. By the end of the day the death toll had reached 700.

The fighting died out that night, but the next day the General Labor Union called for a strike to protest the previous day's attack. A hundred thousand workers heeded the Communist call, bringing waterfront activity to a standstill. As they marched down a Shanghai street, Kuomintang machine gunners cut loose on them, killing more than 300. This was followed by a house-to-house search for Communists who had escaped.

Strangely enough, the Russian Comintern agents in Wuhan tried to bring about an understanding with Chiang despite this coup against the Chinese Communist Party. The Fifth Conference of the Communist Party was hastily called. It convened in Wuhan in May. Chen Tu-hsiu was still head of the Party. Borodin and M. H. Roy, the Indian Communist, with several others, including the American Communist, Earl Browder, represented the Comintern.

Mao Tse-tung pushed his proposals for land reform, which would insure the peasants' support of the Communist Party.

Chen Tu-hsiu refused to allow Mao's suggestions to be considered by the Central Committee. In his autobiography, Mao said, "My opinions were not even discussed."

Mao now realized that the Communist Party was breaking up. He moved to take advantage of the situation. Immediately following the Communist conference, Mao set about organizing the All-China Peasants' Union, with himself as president. Chen was struggling desperately to repair the break between the Kuomintang and the Communist Party that had been brought about by the Shanghai massacre. He was furious to learn that Mao was again stirring up the Hunanese peasants. Mao said, "Chen Tu-hsiu had withdrawn me from Hunan, holding me responsible for certain happenings there, and violently opposed my ideas."

The "certain happenings" that Mao mentioned were insurrections Mao mounted against some of the richer landlords, which resulted in the final collapse of the Wuhan government. A meeting of the Communist Party deposed Chen. Borodin and the other Russian advisors hastily returned to Russia. Borodin somehow survived Stalin's purges but never again was given a position of international responsibility.

The collapse almost destroyed the Communist Party in China, but it marked the beginning of Mao's climb to the top.

His advance was neither easy nor rapid. It took twenty-two years and was filled with narrow escapes, wild adventure, and bitter fights with his enemies in the Kuomintang and the Communist Party alike. He was expelled by the Communist Party and at one time placed under house arrest. A hundred times he faced extermination by Chiang Kai-shek's troops. But in every case he somehow managed to survive and came back to confound his enemies both in and out of his party.

6

The Bandits of Chingkanshan

The Shanghai Massacre and the breakup of the coalition government at Wuhan were a devastating blow to the Chinese Communist Party, but not a fatal one. With the blundering Russian influence temporarily removed, the Chinese radicals moved on three separate fronts. It is a matter of controversy whether the three fronts cooperated with each other.

The first was an uprising in Nanchang in Kiangsi Province, almost due east of Changsha in Hunan. Li Li-san and Chou En-lai seem to have been the prime movers, with help from Chu Teh, the ex-Kuomintang general who became commander-in-chief of the Red Army. Mao told Edgar Snow that he had no part in the uprising in any capacity. Agnes Smedley quotes Chu Teh as saying Mao did attend the planning sessions, but he admitted that he did not see Mao himself.

The conspirators formed a Front Committee—a field force to direct the uprising. Liu Po-cheng was elected chairman, with Chou En-lai as vice-chairman. Among the later famous names on the committee, in addition to Li Li-san, were Chang Kuo-tao, Ho Lung, and Lo Mai. Some sources claim that Chang Kuo-tao bitterly opposed the uprising. In any event, the uprising was a failure. The Red Army under Chu Teh got no support from the workers in the city, nor from the peasants along the way. The failure of the peasants to support them was a surprise to Chu Teh, and it was this failure that later caused him to accept Mao Tse-tung's leadership.

While the fighting was still going on in Nanchang, Mao Tse-Tung was working feverishly to bring about his own uprising in Changsha. The different versions of what happened contradict each other. Basically, however, Mao was trying to bring about what he had outlined in a "Report on an Investigation of the Agrarian Movement in Hunan," which had appeared in the *Communist Guide Weekly* in March 1927. It was a passionate cry for the Party to recognize the peasant as a revolutionary force.

"The force of the peasantry," he wrote, "is like that of raging winds and driving rain. It is rapidly increasing in violence. No force can stand in its way. The peasantry will tear apart all ropes that bind them from taking the road of liberation. They will bury all forces of imperialism, militarism, corrupt officials, village bosses and evil gentry . . . . Shall we stand in the vanguard and lead them or stand behind them and oppose them?"

In organizing the peasants for revolt, Mao told Edgar Snow that he had the permission of the Hunan Provincial Committee, but he was opposed by the Communist Party Central Committee. The attack, which came to be known as the Autumn Harvest Uprising, began on September 5, 1927, with a drive on Ping Kiang, northeast of Changsha. Mao, as chairman of the Front Committee, was the political commissar and actual strategic director, although the army commander was Lu Te-ming.

It was a small army, numbering only four regiments. Two of the regiments were made up of Kuomintang deserters, including some Whampoa cadets. One regiment was comprised of the hard-fighting, hard-bitten miners who had originally been organized by Li Li-san. The fourth regiment was made up of peasants, and Mao Tse-tung personally commanded it, besides carrying on his political work.

The Mao army drove south, capturing three towns and many supplies. Then it turned west and drove on Changsha. Peasants flocked to Mao's banner. Some he outfitted with captured guns; others were armed with pitchforks and scythes from their farms, and with makeshift spears. They were not really fighting for Communism, which most of them did not understand; they were fighting for Mao's promised land reform. Mao's plan called for confiscation of big estates owned by absentee landlords and for taking away surplus land which smaller farmers could not farm themselves. The latter would have included Mao's father. The confiscated property would be divided among the landless tenants.

The Nanchang uprising failed because it depended on a provisional army and the working class. Mao achieved initial success in his Autumn Harvest Uprising because he drew support from the peasant class that had refused to join the Nanchang revolt. The farmers of Nanchang had looked upon Chu Teh's Red Army as just another warlord army.

However, Mao made the same mistake the Nanchang planners had made, but in the opposite direction. Nanchang failed because the peasants were not organized; Mao failed because he did nothing to gain the support of the industrial workers in Changsha. He had assumed that they would cripple the city with strikes, as workers had done in Shanghai to aid Chiang Kai-shek the previous April. Skilled organizers like Chou En-lai had worked hard to give the Shanghai workers a sense of purpose, but Changsha had no organizer.

If the proletariat and the peasant factions of the Party had cooperated, there is a strong possibility that they could have won the struggle ten years earlier than they did. At that time it was impossible for the revolutionists to mass and supply an army large enough to defeat Chiang Kai-shek in battle. Their strategy was to attack with a small revolutionary army, which would then be augmented by masses of the oppressed, flocking to join it as it swept from one victory to another.

That did not happen, either at Nanchang or at Changsha in Mao's Autumn Harvest Uprising. Each revolt was headed by a group interested in appealing only to a single class and contemptuous of the other class. The Russian-dominated branch of the Chinese Communist Party was wrong in its assumption that if they organized the industrial workers and took the cities, then the docile peasants would fatalistically bow to the new government, which would be a dictatorship of the proletariat.

Mao's early victories in the Autumn Harvest Uprising were due to his attacks on small cities and towns that were predominantly rural. There the people responded because they knew him and what he stood for. The situation turned sour as he approached industrialized urban Changsha. The workers did not believe in Mao Tse-tung. They did not hamper the defense by crippling strikes and wild riots as they had in Shanghai. Land reform meant nothing to them, and there were no organizers to tell them that Mao would see that their three dollars a month salaries would be raised and their working conditions improved.

Two of Mao's regiments were made up of a large number of Kuomintang army deserters. As resistance stiffened, Kuomintang secret agents began working among the deserters. One regiment, promised amnesty by the agents, turned on the other regiment. Since Mao only had four regiments in all, this eliminated half his force. Instead of pausing to regroup and settle the trouble, Mao pressed on. He was sure that everyone in Changsha would come to his aid.

Mao operated as chairman of the Front Committee which directed the operation. He kept moving between the two remaining units as they plunged recklessly toward Changsha in order to coordinate their actions. One was a peasant regiment and the other was made up predominantly of miners from Hanyang. On one of his shuttle trips between the two regiments, Mao and the squad with him ran into a *min-tuan* ambush. Min-tuan were mercenary provincial troops hired by rich landlords to protect their property.

Mao was caught in the open. He would have been shot down if he had run. So he surrendered, hoping he could bribe the poorly paid soldiers to let him go. Unfortunately for Mao, the officer in charge of the ambush was incorruptible. He ordered his men to take the prisoner back to their head-quarters.

Mao's situation was desperate. They had not yet identified him as the notorious rebel Mao Tse-tung, but that made little difference. The Kuomintang commander in Changsha was executing all Communists rebels who fell into his hands anyway.

Mao dropped his head and shuffled along with his guards as if he had given up hope. However, he kept cutting his eyes around at his captors, seeking the slightest indication of inat-tention. There was none. They watched him closely. Their guns were pointed straight at his back.

The guards did not relax until they approached the min-tuan headquarters. Mao says they were within two hundred yards before they dropped their rifle barrels. He was now in the enemy camp. Soldiers were all around him. His chances of getting away seemed small indeed. Nevertheless, death on the run was preferable to kneeling docilely while the executioner's sword fell on his bared neck.

He suddenly broke and ran, dodging around the corner of a building and then plunging into a ravine leading toward a pond in the distance. He ducked low, crawling behind some ripening rice, and made for high ground above the pond. There tall, rank grass grew in profusion. He plunged in, snaking his way along the ground to avoid detection.

Behind him the pursuing guards fired several ineffective shots. "The soldiers forced some peasants to help search for me. Many times they came very near, once or twice so close that I could almost have touched them, but somehow I escaped discovery," Mao said later.

One can suppose that Mao owed his escape to the fact that the soldiers forced the farmers to help in the search. Hating the Kuomintang as they did, they naturally were not eager to betray Mao to the min-tuan searchers. If the soldiers had spread out themselves and made the search, they would surely have found the hidden man.

Mao stayed hidden in the tall grass until it became dark, then he started walking toward the mountains. He was barefooted, for he had left his shoes with his regiment in order to look more like a peasant if he were stopped. He was not used to walking on such rocky roads, and his feet were soon bruised and bleeding. He walked all night. Then he met a peasant who helped him get back to what was left of his small army. He found that the peasant and miner regiments had run into ambushes as he had. Their ranks were riddled. The other two, made up of Kuomintang deserters, had mostly deserted again.

Mao was used to setbacks. Undaunted, he reorganized what men he had left into the best semblance of a fighting force he could achieve. He then began retreating south, fighting his way out of first one and then another Kuomintang trap as he headed for a famous bandits' sanctuary, Chingkanshan (Ching-kan Mountain) on the Kiangsi-Hunan border.

The spirit went out of the rebel army as it retreated. The military commander himself deserted. He was replaced by another, who deserted later. The men also slipped away in the night, until Mao reached Chingkanshan with somewhat less than one thousand men. Robert Payne claims that the idea for retreating to Chingkanshan came from Mao's recollection of a bandit leader seeking a similar sanctuary on a mountain in *All Men Are Brothers*, the book Mao had so revered in his youth.

Chingkanshan was not deserted. It was occupied by two famous bandits named Yuan and Wang, who had six hundred men under their combined commands and about two thousand peasant partisans they could call upon when they needed them. The bandits lived mostly by putting a tax on landowners. If the tribute was refused, Yuan and Wang swooped down out of the mountain, burning, looting and seizing men for ransom.

Mao was in a difficult position. Chingkanshan, as described by Robert Payne, was "wildly romantic, with its great forests of pine and spruce and bamboo . . . desolate little paths led into the heart of the mountain fastness . . . And for a greater part of the year the whole area was hidden in fog and mists."

It was also a volcanic peak with extremely rugged cliffs and defiles that made it impregnable against outside attack. Mao could not force his way into that wilderness. He had to negotiate with Wang and Yuan. The bandit chiefs had never been part of the revolutionary movement. Mao did not know how they would receive his request to share their retreat with his defeated army.

Mao's situation was desperate. He hoped to hold on to the few soldiers he had. They would be a cadre around which to rebuild, and Chingkanshan could provide him a sanctuary where the rebuilding could take place. Mao hoped to be able to draw dissidents, Kuomintang deserters and Communist sympathizers into his ranks. Then, after they reached a certain number, he envisioned making guerrilla attacks against towns and cities in the area around the great mountain. These he hoped to group into a soviet, which he could rule as the warlords ruled their provinces. Later that soviet would be expanded until eventually all China would be under his control. Soviet actually means "council" in Russian, and a soviet technically means a governing council. However, in effect it refers to a Communist state.

Mao met with Wang and Yuan. He had to use all his powers of persuasion in his negotiations with the suspicious bandit chiefs. He was arguing for his life, his army, and his dreams. In his teens he had dreamed of becoming a great leader, as his friend Siao-Yu pointed out. Now Mao saw a great opportunity in the collapse of the Chinese Communist Party. He was convinced that this had come about because of the Party's reliance on Russian advisors who did not understand that conditions in China differed from those in Russia. He felt now that if he could establish a soviet state, he could use it as a base for defeating his enemies in and out of the party. The result would lead him to dominance in China.

After some sharp negotiating, Wang and Yuan agreed to let Mao's hungry, ragged troops march into their stronghold. In light of what came after, it would appear that the two bandit chiefs thought they could eventually eliminate Mao and absorb his men into their own ranks. As it was, they agreed to consolidate their six hundred men with Mao's one thousand, but on condition that their men would comprise a separate group under their own command. The situation promised future conflict, but at the moment Mao had to take the best deal he could make.

In the meantime, the rest of the Chinese Communist Party was experiencing one defeat after another. The group involved in the Nanchang uprising traveled south under Chu Teh and met a crushing defeat at Swatow. Chu Teh reorganized the survivors and—to escape total destruction—headed toward Chingkanshan, where he hoped to unite with Mao Tse-tung.

While Chu Teh was having his troubles, Communists in Canton launched their own revolt. They called it the Canton Commune, but Canton Slaughter would have been a better name for it. It proved a bloody fiasco for the Party. The Party leaders naturally needed someone to blame, and they picked Mao Tse-tung. In November the Party held a Plenum. Mao was denounced both by Li Li-san and Chu Chiu-pai. Chu followed the Russian line by claiming that a peasant uprising that was not led by the proletariat could not expect to win victories. He held Mao's Autumn Harvest Uprising up as an example. He was vigorously supported by Heinz Neumann,

Stalin's envoy to the meeting. They also denounced Mao for dealing with bandits (Wang and Yuan) instead of revolutionaries.

The Central Committee, while blaming others as well, held Mao primarily guilty of breach of Party discipline. The report of the Chinese Communist Party Central Committee said that the Central Committee had sent Mao to Hunan as a Special Commissioner to reorganize the Hunan Provincial Committee. "He was in fact the core of the Hunan Provincial Committee," the angry report went on. "Therefore Comrade Mao should shoulder the most serious responsibility for the mistakes made by the Hunan Provincial Committee."

The Committee then removed Mao from his position as a member of the Politburo of the Central Committee and from the Front Committee. Mao paid no attention to his repudiation by the Central Committee. He continued to enlarge the army he brought to Chingkanshan and enforced strong discipline. After his last two commanders deserted, Mao himself took command in the dual role of military commander and political commissar.

Mao's account of what happened to the bandits Wang and Yuan is at odds with Agnes Smedley's melodramatic account of Chingkanshan. Mao told Edgar Snow that the two were faithful Communists "while I remained on Chingkanshan, and carried out orders of the party." After Mao left, he says, they reverted to banditry and were killed by peasants they raided. Agnes Smedley tells a melodramatic story of how Wang and Yuan were continually in conflict with the Red Army. She claims Yuan was killed by his own troops when he tried to lead them in desertion to the Kuomintang.

Miss Smedley, while denying being a Communist herself, was the most enthusiastic admirer the Red Army ever had. She surpassed Mao himself. And her admiration for General Chu Teh was nothing short of hero worship. There is no denying that she knew the Red Army; she actually lived and marched with it. However, her accounts are highly colored, often melodramatic, and so biased that it is difficult to get a clear overall view from them.

She does, however, give some very interesting vignettes of Red Army life. One of these shows the consternation of the exbandits when Mao set new rules for the Red Army. One of the rules strictly prohibited looting by Red Army soldiers. Anything taken from peasants had to be paid for. Anything confiscated from rich landowners had to be turned into the general Red Army treasury. This was done to gain the support of the peasants to the Red Army cause. While infraction of some of the rules merited surprisingly lenient punishment, looting from peasants was a sure way to face a firing squad.

Miss Smedley quotes one old bandit as saying: "You say we will be shot if we take things from people. Then why do we fight? Never has any man heard of such injustice!"

When told that they were fighting for the revolution, he retorted, "What is this thing Revolution if we fight and die for nothing?"

Mao Tse-tung was well aware of this attitude and its dangers to his revolution. He knew that there was justice in Karl Marx's belief that peasants would fight only until their own wrongs were righted and then stop there, without regard for the full sweep of a revolt. His solution was total indoctrination, or, as he called it, "political instruction." If an army was to be held together with full morale, political indoctrination was as important as basic military training. He believed that men who were properly convinced of the justice of their cause would not have deserted, as so many members of his Autumn Harvest Uprising had done.

At that point Mao was acting as military commander. The army was under attack by Kuomintang forces almost constantly. While Chiang Kai-shek's soldiers and those of the provincial min-tuan could not break through the Chingkanshan defenses, Mao was kept busy planning his defenses. This did not give him time to work out his plans for political instruction of his troops, nor for the theoretical planning he wanted to do about the future of his total program. He was looking for a military commander but could not find a suitable one in his entire force. The two best commanders had deserted to the Kuomintang during the bloody retreat to Chingkanshan.

He found his man finally in May, 1928. It was Chu Teh, who after his defeat at Swatow maneuvered as best he could and then brought his shattered forces to Chingkanshan. As Chu Teh approached the mountain sanctuary, Mao Tse-tung went out to meet him. They knew of each other but had never met. However, they hit it off well from the beginning, becoming so close that they became known as "Chu-Mao," the double man.

With the troops he led at Namchang and Swatow, Chu Teh also had experienced desertions and lack of will to fight. He had arrived at the same conclusion as Mao: political instruction was essential to victory. On that common ground Chu and Mao planned a division of authority, sealing a collaboration that would become legendary.

In Chu Teh Mao found not only the general he sought but also one of the most remarkable military commanders China ever knew. Chu was born in 1886 of a well-to-do and apparently politically important family. Later Communist biographers, assuming that it was necessary for all Red leaders to be of peasant birth, manufactured a poor family for him to be born into. His education was good enough to help him pass the Imperial Manchu civil service examination by the time he was twenty. He quit this in 1908 to enroll in the Yunnan Provincial Military Academy.

He then fought with the local warlord, Tsi Ao, for Sun Yat-sen in the 1911 Revolution. Four years later, Chu Teh had been promoted on ability to brigadier general under Tsai Ao. Then in 1916 the three people who meant the most to Chu Teh—his young wife, his beloved commander, and a man who was his best friend—all died within a short time of each other. Chu Teh became very morose and an opium addict. At the same time he was given greater military responsibilities. Graft permitted him to build a palatial mansion with a harem of concubines.

By 1922 opium had so clouded his mind that he began to lose battles. At that point he suddenly provided support for his wife and concubines, resigned from the army, and went first to Shanghai and then to Germany. There Chou En-lai introduced him into the Chinese Communist Party cell in Berlin. Later he spent some time in France and then returned to China. Chu was now a secret Communist, although he accepted a general's commission in the Kuomintang army. He was later appointed Commissioner for Public Safety in Nanchang. He conspired with the Communists while in that position and during the Namchang Uprising he openly went over to their side. After the Communist defeats at Namchang and Swatow, he joined Mao Tse-tung at Chingkanshan.

Now while Chu Teh molded the bandits, Mao's troops and his own into a new army, Mao Tse-tung made his plans for developing the area around Chingkanshan into a soviet. The entire plan was doomed, however, and before long the "bandits of Chingkanshan," as Chiang Kai-shek termed them, would be fighting desperately to get out of what turned into a mountain trap.

In the meantime, the rest of the Communist Party was struggling to rebuild itself. Various leaders were trying to pull together armies to establish their own soviets. In the Central Committee Li Li-san, with Russian support, was emerging as the dominant leader. He joined with Hsiang Chung-fa and Chou En-lai to oust Chu Chiu-pai as head of the Party in China. Li Li-san had gone to Russian in 1927 and returned in 1928, claiming a "mandate" from Stalin. This mandate was summed up in a Party report in October 1928, which said that the Party "recognizes that there is a danger that the base of our party may shift from the working class to the peasantry and that we must make every effort to restore the party's working-class base."

This was a clear warning to Mao Tse-tung that his efforts to form a peasant-based soviet did not have the party's sanction. The party would follow the Li Li-san line devoted to organizing urban workers.

So, although the party restored Mao to a position in the Central Committee in late 1928, the battle lines were drawn between the leaders and the Red Rebel of Chingkanshan.

7
Mao's Bandits

While Li Li-san brought in his henchmen to high positions in the party as part of an attempt to make himself the Chinese Stalin, Mao Tse-tung planned and schemed to build a soviet around Chingkanshan. Both men moved for power too soon with too little to back their ambitions. As a result, both had their dreams shattered.

Mao's defeat came first. Chingkanshan just wasn't large enough to support his growing army. Claims by some writers that the mountain meadows could grow three rice crops a year simply is not true. The farms on the mountain, together with what the bandits grabbed on their raids, were sufficient for the bandits who hid there before the coming of the Communists. After Mao arrived with a thousand men, to be joined later by another thousand under Chu Teh, and still another thousand under General Peng Teh-huai, a Kuomintang deserter who had previously served under Chu Teh, the resources of the mountain retreat were insufficient to feed them all.

The situation worsened in the winter of 1928. They existed only by raiding rich landowners, holding them for ransom, and using the money to buy foodstuffs from farmers. Then Chiang Kai-shek was able to make deals with some of the warlords he had been fighting. This permitted him to release a large contingent of troops from his Northern Campaign. They came south to fight the "red bandits" of Chingkanshan.

Chiang's Nationalist Kuomintang army could not storm the mountain itself. He began a siege. The Communists' ammunition and other military supplies and equipment were running low, for their only resupply came from what they could capture from the enemy. For lack of ammunition, they dug pits in the trails, stuck bamboo stakes upright in the bottoms, and then covered the tops of the pits with grass so the Kuomintang soldiers advancing along the trails would fall in and be impaled. They moved huge boulders to the top of cliffs so they could be rolled down on the enemy. Many, according to what Chu Teh told Agnes Smedley, made bows and arrows. In one case they hollowed a log and packed the inside with powder and rock. The improvised cannon was pointed down a rocky road and used to blast an advancing enemy company.

Mao later told Edgar Snow that food was so scarce that they practically lived on squash. The soldiers kept their sense of humor despite their worsening condition, for Mao reported that their battle cry was, "Down with capitalism—and eat squash!"

The Kuomintang no longer attempted to storm the mountain. Instead they drew a tight siege line around it and settled down to starve the Reds out. Agnes Smedley described the conditions on Chingkanshan: "Men shivered in their threadbare cotton garments. With each passing week they became more gaunt. They struggled with hunger and they struggled with lice." Those who complained were scornfully told, "You can go back to being a landlord's slave or shut your mouth."

Despite the unquestioned heroism of their men, Mao and Chu Teh realized that they would all die unless they left the mountain. Sickness was killing more of the soldiers than the enemy was. So Mao, Chu Teh and Peng Teh-huai held a serious strategy conference in a back room of a Buddhist monastery the Reds had taken over high among the rocks of Chingkanshan.

They hunched over a map of South China while they schemed, argued and planned for the future. They all agreed on leaving Chingkanshan. That was imperative. Ho Lung, who had fought with Chu Teh at Namchang, was trying to carve out a soviet republic in north Hunan, but Mao rejected the idea of trying to join him. He felt that the area would not support a larger group than Ho Lung then had under his control. Also, he did not want to join someone else. He had not been wasting the months at Chingkanshan after Chu Teh had taken over direction of the fighting for him. He had worked all the days and most of the nights over his maps and plans for the organization of his own soviet. This would be a republic in which he could express his own variations of Marxism.

Chu Teh did not really care where they went as long as the area was defensible militarily. All his arguments were based solely on that consideration. Mao, in turn, felt that their operations should be in deeply agrarian sectors where the peasants were particularly oppressed by rapacious landlords. There the Red Army would be able to draw support from a large group of partisans.

Also, the landlords were essential to Mao's plans for financing his operations. Where most Chinese armies lived off the land by looting everybody, Mao was determined that his army would respect the peasants' right of property in order to gain their support. All necessary looting—and they had no other way to support themselves—would be carried on against the landlord and merchant classes.

Mao's idea was to break out of the iron ring of soldiers surrounding Chingkanshan and to maneuver into southeast Kiangsi province in an area near the Fukien border. This would put them in the center of a circular area bounded by

Foochow, on the coast of the East China Sea; Canton, to the south and separated from them by the Nanling Mountains; Namchang to the north; and Changsha, in adjoining Hunan province, to the northwest. Thus there would be hotbeds of Communist sympathizers and activity on all sides of them to distract Chiang Kai-shek and the provincial warlords from throwing their concentrated force against the soviet Mao hoped to build in the Kiangsi-Fukien mountain area.

Chu Teh agreed that the terrain would be ideal for guerrilla warfare. The hills and valleys and the timber would give him plenty of opportunity to strike at any pursuing enemy from many directions. Then the attacking forces could split into small groups and melt into the rough terrain. If the enemy broke his own ranks to pursue, the Reds, knowing the land, could easily cut them to pieces.

Peng Teh-huai's army had been the last to arrive on Chingkanshan and had not regained its strength. So the three planners decided that Peng and Wang, the ex-bandits, would remain on the mountain. With the others gone, the food and supply situation would be somewhat eased. The presence of a portion of the Red Army there would also force Chiang Kai-shek to retain a sizeable number of troops to counter the threat. This would cut down the number of his men who would be pursuing Mao and Chu Teh.

The strategy called for Peng Teh-huai to make a feint down the main road from the mountains. The leaders of the Kuomintang blockade pulled troops from other areas to reenforce those they expected to be attacked. Then Mao and Chu brought their four thousand soldiers down back trails, regrouped, and slammed through the enemy blockade lines at a weak point.

The move confused the Nationalist Kuomintang commanders. Unable to decide which front was the main one, they made the mistake of concentrating on Peng Teh-huai, so that Mao and Chu Teh made a clean breakthrough with a surprisingly small loss. Peng then retreated back into the shelter of Chingkanshan's volcanic cliffs.

During the first critical days of the breakthrough, Mao and Chu Teh demonstrated the perfect harmony in action that was responsible for their becoming known as Chu-Mao and thought of as a single man rather then two people.

In time the name "Chu-Mao" was used so often to describe the leader of the ghostly guerrilla bands who struck through Kiangsi that foreign newspapermen became confused. Often their dispatches to Europe and the United States would read, "General Chu-Mao, the notorious Red bandit, attacked the Nationalist stronghold in . . . ." Some of the reporters never learned that Chu-Mao was two men, one a brilliant guerrilla leader and the other a political genius who would someday rule the entire Chinese nation.

At Nanchang, Chu Teh had seen that men will not fight well unless they have been strongly indoctrinated politically so that they believe totally in the things they are fighting for. Otherwise, they fight halfheartedly, break and run when the battle becomes fierce, and desert at the first opportunity. Mao Tse-tung had a fire and enthusiasm that was contagious. Mao could give their men something to fight for, and Chu would see that they fought.

Mao knew from bitter experience that men will not long follow a leader who leaves them with empty bellies. The troops' first consideration was to find food as quickly as possible. Then they needed supplies. Since they could not loot the peasant Mao was trying to bring on his side, their only change to eat and rearm themselves was through fighting the enemy.

Once through the enemy lines, Chu Teh swung his men around and smashed into the pursuing enemy from fifty guerrilla positions. Again the Kuomintang generals were afraid to split their forces. Their entire army charged ahead, pursuing only a small force of Communists, who led them into treacherous hills where the rest of the Reds could hit them at their flanks and rear. Then, taking what spoils they captured in food and ammunition, the Red guerrilla bands fled in every direction, to remass later at a predetermined spot.

Once reunited, Mao and Chu Teh led them through narrow mountain defiles deep into Kiangsi. They avoided most urban areas, for those were too well defended. However, they over-ran a mountain mining town, where all the rice stores were taken for the Red Army.

The merchants, mine officials, and rich landowners were herded together and informed that the Red Army had ap-pointed itself tax collector for the district. A tax bill was handed them. (In Agnes Smedley's version the bill was fastened to the end of a bayonet and shoved in the face of the merchants' spokesman.) The victims paid, and paid quickly.

This became the standard pattern for the Red Army's sup-ply and finance departments. Mao received absolutely no help either from the Chinese Communist Party or from the Russians. He and Chu Teh were strictly on their own, snub-bed because Mao refused to follow the Russian and Li Li-san line.

They continued to fight the enemy to capture guns and food. Chu Teh called a battle a victory only if they won plenty of booty. When the rice stores they captured were more than the Red Army could carry away, it was Mao's policy to dis-tribute the surplus to the poor in the district where it was taken. The guerrillas had to keep mobile and could not burden themselves with too many supplies.

In robbing the rich and giving part of the loot to the poor, Mao was following the Robin Hood tradition. While he had never heard of the English folk hero, the bandit heroes of his favorite story, *All Men Are Brothers*, were cast in the Robin Hood mold. In Mao's case, the procedure was good business. He was making friends who would grab guns and fight as par-tisans when the occasion demanded.

In this way the Chu-Mao army, which in time became the Red First Front Army, gradually enlarged its hold on a wide area along the Kiangsi-Fukien border. The Communists were soon able to establish permanent headquarters. Then, in the battle of Tingchow, Chu Teh captured a Kuomintang arsenal and uniform factory. Before he was forced to retreat, he dismantled both. His soldiers carried off the vital machinery on their backs and reassembled it in Communist-held territory.

Chu Teh was happier with the uniform factory than he was with the arsenal. Up to that point the Red Army had dressed in whatever rags the soldiers happened to own. Once they got relocated, Chu Teh got the factory in operation and the Red Army made its first uniforms. They were cut from gray-blue cloth, and each peaked cap had a small red star. "They were not as fine as foreign uniforms, but to us they were very fine indeed," Chu Teh later told Agnes Smedley.

The new uniforms helped to build pride in the soldiers. At the same time, each evening when they were not fighting or fleeing, Mao and his corps of political workers were drumming into them the principles for which they were fighting. Deserters from the Kuomintang were brought out to tell the men about the way they had been treated in Chiang Kai-shek's army—the brutality, the difference in privileges of rank, the lack of consideration. Then a political worker would contrast these things with the democratic ways of the Red Army, where officers and men wore the same uniform, shared the same pay, and ate the same food. Red Army officers were forbidden to curse or mistreat any man, and theoretically the common soldiers were permitted to criticize their officers.

The political indoctrination often turned on Chinese history and how Chiang Kai-shek had chosen to throw his lot with the "foreign devils" who were exploiting the country. The men were reminded of Japanese acts of aggression and the loss of Korea. Then the evening's lessons ended with entertainment. Actors with the political corps put on skits and little plays that satirized capitalism and the enemies of the Communist Party. The final part of the entertainment was sing-songs with all the audience joining in. Sometimes they sang old Chinese folk songs and sometimes Western tunes, but always with new lyrics glorifying some facet of the revolution.

Although Agnes Smedley and some other writers tend to

represent the Red Army as one big happy family devoted to themselves and the Revolution, there were numerous desertions, breaches of discipline, and in at least one case, a serious mutiny. In every case discipline was strict and punishment was swift and sure. Mao showed his toughness a year later when he put down a revolt of 4,400 Red Army troops, shooting their leaders and 400 followers. When force was necessary, Mao Tse-tung could be as ruthless as any man. However, he showed, both in his dealing with the Army and with his fellow Communist leaders, that he preferred persuasion to force.

Throughout 1929 Mao continued to gain strength, but at the same time his relations with the Chinese Communist Party grew worse. Twice Li Li-san wrote Mao through the Central Committee, demanding that he stop "adventurism" among the peasants and direct the Red Army against urban centers where workers could be organized. Mao replied to the first of these letters, disagreeing with Li Li-san on policy and tactics. The second letter Mao ignored.

Li Li-san's high-handed manner earned him many enemies. Chen Tu-hsiu tried to take advantage of this by organizing groups to oppose Li. Li Li-san struck back by forcing the Central Committee to expel Chen and all his followers from the Party. At the same time Li Li-san attempted to settle his differences with Mao. Meanwhile, Mao realized that he was going too far in his rejection of the Party line. Chiang Kai-shek was rapidly consolidating his position and would be able to throw an increased army against the Communist bases.

There was a genuine need for cooperation between the party and its splinter groups. Mao was rapidly enlarging his area in Kiangsi. Ho Lung was trying to carve out a soviet republic in western Hunan, and two other leaders were struggling to do the same thing in other parts of China. Li Li-san's objective was to bring all of these under his control.

The Party leaders met at Kutien in Fukien Province, near Mao's base. It was a mountain town that had recently been captured by Chu Teh. In the course of the conference, Mao agreed to disband the soldier soviets (councils) he had formed in his army, or at least to subordinate their power to a regular political commissariat. It has been suggested that Mao was not actually making a concession to the Central Committee, as it appeared. He had found that the soldier soviets were not working out satisfactorily and that ambitious men were using them in an attempt to build up personal power.

Mao fought hard at the Kutien Conference for a change in the Party line. In years to come when Maoist historians tried to rewrite history to show that Mao had been correct from the beginning, it was noted that he won a victory in his struggle with the Party during this conference. However, the succeeding actions of the Central Committee show that Mao won nothing. Most of the military leaders at the conference stood firm against Mao's plan to establish a soviet republic in the Kiangsi-Fukien region. They did not believe the area could support a permanently based army. They argued strongly for capturing a city, possibly Changsha, which they could use as the Red Army base.

Frustrated in his attempts to control military strategy, Mao had to stand by while the Red Army attempted to follow the Li Li-san line. In July, 1930, Peng Teh-huai—who had been forced out of Chingkanshan four months after Mao and Chu left—attacked Changsha with a Communist army numbering about ten thousand men. Ho Chien, the defending warlord, had 30,000 troops, but their lack of fighting spirit permitted the Communist troops to take the city.

Again the working class failed to rally to the Communist cause. Ho Chien counterattacked with additional reinforcements. Peng Teh-huai was forced to retreat after holding the city for only ten days. Mao and Chu tried to come to his aid but were likewise unsuccessful. The Communists charged that an American gunboat steamed up the Yangtze from Shanghai to aid Ho Chien.

Once back in command in Changsha, Ho Chien began a

reign of terror to destroy all those who had aided the Communists during the ten-day occupation. Hundreds died, both in the city and throughout Hunan. It was sometime during this period that Ho Chien captured Yang Kai-hui, Mao's young wife and she was executed on his direct orders. There is no doubt that Ho Chien, a viciously brutal and cruel man, took delight in executing one close to Mao Tse-tung, but her work organizing youth groups would have earned her the headsman's sword even if she had been an unknown peasant. Chu Teh's wife was also slain in either 1929 or 1930, but she fell in battle.

Changsha was the beginning of the end for Li Li-san. He made a hurried trip to Moscow to bolster support, but in early 1931 he was deposed by party leaders. Mao Tse-tung had hoped to take Li Li-san's place as Party secretary, but he was swept aside by a group known as the "Twenty-eight Bolsheviks." They in turn owed their victory to the Comintern agent Pavel Mif. Leaders of the new faction were "Wang Ming" (Chen Shao-yu) and "Po Ku" (Chin Pang-hsien).

The Twenty-eight Bolsheviks—the derisive name was tacked on by their political enemies in the Communist Party—were young students who had gone to Russia in 1926 to study at the newly opened Sun Yat-sen University in Moscow. Pavel Mif had been one of the school officials. In light of what happened after they returned to China, it is clear that the Russians trained the twenty-eight young Chinese for the specific purpose of taking over the direction of the floundering Chinese Communist Party.

Since they followed the basic Li Li-san line, it also is clear that Li Li-san was deposed not because of the failure of the Changsha attack, which was the official story, but because he had been unable to bring Mao Tse-tung and Chu Teh—leaders of the strongest of the Red armies—under direct Party control.

In Moscow Li Li-san learned of his removal as Party head. There he abjectly confessed his errors and begged Party forgiveness. His Russian masters announced that he was undergoing additional political training.

Back in China, Chou En-lai also made a public confession of his political and theoretical errors. But unlike Li Li-san, Chou En-lai was not publicly disgraced. As leader of the Whampoa faction (made up of graduates of the Whampoa Military Academy organized by Chiang Kai-shek), Chou emerged as chairman of the Party's Military Committee. He soon became Mao's chief adversary.

From this point on, the lives of Mao Tse-tung and Chou En-lai were closely intertwined. Chou, son of a patrician family, had been indocrinated into Communism while a student in Paris and Berlin. He returned to China in 1924 and was employed by Chiang Kai-shek as an instructor at the Whampoa Military Academy. One of his prize students was a stern-faced young man named Lin Piao, who would later become one of the military geniuses of the Red Army and the planner of the Chinese attack on American troops in Korea.

Chou was one of the organizers who stirred up the workers in Shanghai to open the city to Chiang Kai-shek's advance in 1927. After Chiang rejected Communism and conducted the Shanghai massacre, Chou En-lai became one of the leading Communists. From that time to this day, he has never been long outside the ruling hierarchy of the Chinese Communist Party. No one, not even Mao Tse-tung, can match that record. Chou's ability to survive every purge, every change in the party leadership, and every shift of ideology is one of the mysteries of Chinese Communism.

The power struggle within the Chinese Communist Party continued after the Twenty-Eight Bolsheviks assumed power. Wang Ming claimed that Mao was an empirist, interested only in building a kingdom he could rule. Mao in turn contemptuously called the Bolsheviks "Three-Year-Babies," in reference to the fact that their sole revolutionary experience had been three years in Russia's Sun Yat-sen University.

Accounts of the political struggle during this critical time are contradictory and often confusing. The only thing that stands out clearly is that Mao Tse-tung was in definite opposition to the rest of the Chinese Communist Party, but his growing power in Kiangsi forced the Party leaders to treat him more leniently than they would normally have done. They tried on several occasions to make peace with Mao, but he stubbornly held his own course. He could afford to do so because his soviet republic was growing in size, population and power while the others were barely keeping alive.

However, it must be admitted that Mao's success in building up the Kiangsi soviet depended upon Chu Teh's genius as a guerrilla leader. Mao was far from the greatly beloved figure some of his biographers have tried to make him. Descriptions of him during this period call him aloof, moody, and far from popular with anyone but Chu Teh. Pictures show him to be tall, thin and with a dreamy expression more fitting to a poet than a great revolutionist. He was totally oblivious to his personal appearance, dressing in wrinkled pants and a jacket that he wore buttoned to the collar. His thick black hair was parted in the middle and hung bushily on each side of his head.

Chu Teh supplied the popular appeal that Mao lacked. He was completely down-to-earth, always smiling, and friendly with everyone. "Oh, everybody likes Chu Teh," his wife told the writer Nym Wales. She said it in the same tone one would say, "The sun is shining," as if it was so obvious that no one could possible doubt it. And she was very close to right.

Even within his own group Mao encountered opposition. Quite possibly much of it was secretly inspired by the Twenty-Eight Bolsheviks to undermine Mao's power. It is known that overtures were made to Chu Teh to break away from the Maoist group. Chu Teh refused, without betraying the plotters to Mao. In later years little incidents would come out indicating that the Chu-Mao leadership was not as close as everyone thought. However, each leader recognized the other's ability, and realized that the two of them together had a strength than neither could achieve alone.

After settling his protegés in power, Pavel Mif returned to Moscow, where he became head of the Chinese Section of the Comintern. His job was to see that Russian support kept the Twenty-Eight Bolsheviks in power. Mao, who had rejected Stalinism and the Russian brand of Marxism, worked to undermine the new Party leaders. The Comintern undertook a campaign to destroy Mao. The first attack took the form of an order for the Red Army to stop guerrilla warfare and consolidate for attacks on industrial cities.

Mao discussed the order with Chu Teh, contemptuously observing that the deposition of Li Li-san had not changed the Li Li-san line at all. Chu Teh agreed. Previously the Chinese Communist Party had nearly destroyed itself in futile attacks on the larger cities, while Mao and Chu had gained strength by abandoning the proletariat for the peasant.

Next, the Comintern attacked Mao's land policy in his Kiangsi soviet. Mao had not abolished private ownership of land but had actually protected some landowners of the middle class. Only the land of the very rich had been confiscated and divided among the very poor. Mao understood the peasants' love of the land. He knew he could not hold their support at that critical time if he abolished private ownership of land as true Marxism demanded.

This lenient policy, plus Chu Teh's military genius, permitted Mao Tse-tung to build his soviet republic into the largest in China and the second largest outside the Soviet States of Russia. At the height of the Kiangsi soviet Mao claimed to control eighteen million people.

His accomplishment should have earned Mao the respect of the entire Communist world. Instead, it only intensified the power struggle. Inevitably it led to disaster for the Chinese Communist Party, its leaders, and for Mao Tse-tung.

After the debacle was over, only Mao, Chu Teh and the indestructible Chou En-lai had the strength to climb back to power.

8

The Long March

During 1931 Chiang Kai-shek launched three "Red Bandit Extermination Campaigns," with each one quickly following the other. He made progress against the Communist soviets in some areas but failed to dislodge Mao and Chu from Kiangsi. Mao continued to build his Communist republic. He adopted a constitution, elected himself president, collected taxes, and became the Communist Party's greatest financial backer. Still he could not control the Party.

In the meantime, Chiang Kai-shek had to postpone his Fourth Red Bandit Extermination Campaign, which he hoped would destroy Mao. The Japanese had attacked Manchuria and later made an attack on Shanghai. Mao and Chu called for united Chinese action against the Japanese and even went so far as to have their soviet declare war on the invaders.

Chiang continued to feel that Mao and Chu were more dangerous to him than the Japanese. He hastened to appease the Japanese as best he could, so he could resume his attack on

Mao Tse-tung's Kiangsi soviet. The Fourth Extermination Campaign lasted eight months, beginning in June 1932 and dragging on until February 1933. Like the previous three campaigns, it failed to dislodge Mao and Chu.

The days of Mao's soviet republic were numbered anyway, but its greatest danger was Mao's enemies in the Party. In August, 1932, in the third month of the Fourth Extermination Campaign, the Party leaders met at Ningtu for a conference. Chou En-lai argued strongly that the Red Army needed to cease operating in small guerrilla bands. It should mass into a one-million-man army that would be strong enough to sweep across China. Mao was ill, suffering from malaria complicated by exhaustion, but still he tried to fight. He was dismayed when Peng Teh-huai joined Chu Teh in agreeing with Chou En-lai.

Abandoned by his generals, Mao had to sweat and shake in his malarial bed while the Twenty-Eight Bolsheviks, aided by Chou En-lai, took over the military direction of Mao's First Front Army.

Chou En-lai, a man of tremendous ability and surprising ways, then came to Mao's aid. A resolution condemning Mao as a rightist and demanding his expulsion from the party was introduced at the conference by Wang Ming. It would have passed but for the strong objections of Chou En-lai and Chu Teh.

This backing did not prevent Chou from agreeing—and even pushing—to have Mao removed from his position on the party's Military Committee. Chou became chairman of the Military Committee with headquarters in Mao's capital city of Juichin. His responsibility was similar to that of the Secretary of Defense in the United States government. Theoretically Chou was superior in the party to Mao and all the generals. Thus Chou received credit in party circles for preventing Chiang Kai-shek's Fourth Extermination Campaign from breaking into the Kiangsi soviet republic.

The Western Hunan Soviet of the ex-bandit Ho Lung also

remained intact, but other elements of the Communist Party were badly mauled in the campaign. The Central Committee, which had its headquarters in Shanghai, had to flee to Kiangsi. The Maoist version of the story is that they came there at the invitation of Mao Tse-tung. The reasoning behind the invitation was to bring the Central Committee into Kiangsi where Mao could dominate it.

Unfortunately for this claim, Mao Tse-tung was in no position to dominate anybody. He was still sick, cared for by the noted doctor Nelson Fu and nursed by his wife, Ho Tzu-chen, whom he had married after the execution of Yang Kai-hui. Mao's illness, plus the wavering support of his generals, had permitted Chou En-lai to weaken Mao's power greatly in the Kiangsi soviet. The arrival of the Central Committee with the top leaders of the Chinese Communist Party strengthened Chou En-lai's position and further weakened Mao.

Mao now had to stand aside futilely while the Twenty-Eight Bolsheviks, in association with Chou En-lai's Whampoa clique, stole the republic that Mao's political adroitness and Chu Teh's fighting genius had built. Wang Ming, the short, fat little man who had emerged as party head after Li Li-san was deposed, did not choose to flee to Juichin. He went to Moscow to join his mentor, Pavel Mif, in the Far East Section of the Comintern. Po Ku succeeded him as Party Secretary. At that time the Party Secretary outranked the Chairman.

It had been Wang Ming's intention, supported by Po Ku and Chou En-lai, to band the Red Army guerrilla units into a mass army as soon as Mao Tse-tung's opposition was overcome. It would then be used for attacking Chiang Kai-shek's army directly and seizing cities as additional power bases. This was a direct return to the Stalin-supported Li Li-san line. To help reorganize the Red Army along this line, the Comintern smuggled the German Communist Otto Braun into Kiangsi. Chiang Kai-shek had brought in German military advisers to direct his Fifth Red Bandit Extermination Campaign, and Braun was brought in as their Communist counterpart. General Von Seekt, who planned the siege for Chiang, pulled a blockade line of a million men around the Kiangsi soviet. Instead of direct attacks, which Chu Teh could counter with guerrilla tactics as usual, Von Seekt constructed a series of stone blockhouses that could not be reduced by guerrilla bands. They could be taken only by direct frontal assault backed by artillery, which the defending Red Army did not have.

Von Seekt taught Chiang Kai-shek to be patient. Before, Chiang had launched three Extermination Campaigns one after another within the space of a single year. Now the Kuomintang moved slowly, building blockhouses and then advancing to build a new ring of stone and steel. This not only started to squeeze Mao's Kiangsi republic but also left blockhouses in depth so that the Red Army could not filter through. Even more important, it prevented the Communists from bringing in badly needed supplies. While Mao had an arsenal in Juichin, it could not operate without raw materials. It was used mostly for ordnance repair. The Red Army supply system depended primarily, as it always had, upon materiel captured from the enemy. The blockhouse system of attack very effectively cut the amount of captured guns and ammunition Chu Teh could obtain.

All concerned—enemy, Communist and Russian advisors—realized that this was a new type of warfare for the Red Army, something it could not cope with. Even Chu Teh agreed that the guerrilla tactics he and the Red Army knew best could not fight the stone fortresses that Von Seekt had built. The Mao republic was slowly being strangled. As a result, none of the Chinese generals objected when the Comintern smuggled Otto Braun in from Canton.

Braun was a product of the Imperial German Army and had joined the German Communist Party in the 1920s. He was a burly man, with the typical Prussian military arrogance. The Comintern, in an attempt to conceal from Von Seekt the identity of his adversary, gave Braun the cover name of Li Teh. This maneuver was so successful that Li Teh's true identity was not revealed for many years. As late as 1950 writers were referring to him as Li Teh, the mysterious German general.

Mao detested Li Teh from the beginning. They were exact opposites. Mao was conciliatory. He never used force until every effort at persuasion ended. He could fight an enemy ruthlessly but forgive and accept that enemy into his own force once the enemy was defeated. He cared nothing for personal comforts, living and eating no better than the lowest ranking soldier in the ranks. The one notable exception was that he smoked heavily, although Red Army rules discouraged smoking among the soldiers.

Li Teh, on the other hand, was overbearing, blunt and authoritative in giving orders and insisted on communistically untypical privileges for himself. He insisted that a man of his bulk could not get along on a single ration; he wanted two. He also decided that he was lonely and demanded a Chinese girl friend. This scandalized Mao, who was somewhat puritannical.

However, Li Teh was their great military hope. Po Ku was his great patron and served as Li Teh's personal translator. At the same time Po Ku and his Twenty-Eight Bolsheviks, in collaboration with Chou En-lai and his Whampoa Clique, systematically began purging Maoist sympathizers from top positions throughout the Kiangsi soviet. Whispers in Party ranks claimed that Mao Tse-tung would soon be as politically dead as the discredited Li Li-san.

While this intraparty struggle went on, the Kuomintang blockade was drawn tighter by Von Seekt and the Kuomintang Army. Communist ammunition stocks were being depleted at an alarming rate. Food stocks were still adequate, but the shortage of salt was serious. Salt is a human necessity. None was produced in Kiangsi. It had to be imported from salt wells in Hunan or from evaporation beds along the coast of Fukien Province. The Kuomintang blockade had effectively dammed both sources.

The situation for the Communists was moving toward

disaster when the Kuomintang Nineteenth Route Army suddenly revolted in Fukien Province in October 1933. The Nineteenth Route Army had opposed the Japanese attack on Shanghai in 1932, holding back the invaders for two months before they had to retreat.

Then instead of reequipping the Nineteenth for a counterattack, Chiang signed an armistice that permitted Japanese occupation troops to remain in Shanghai. This truce permitted Chiang to resume his Extermination Campaign against the Kiangsi soviet. The Nineteenth Route Army generals bitterly denounced Chiang for continuing to fight his fellow Chinese while the "dwarf bandits" of Japan stole Chinese cities.

The rebels set up a "People's Government" at Foochow on the Fukien coast and asked the Communists for cooperation against Chiang. Po Ku refused to take any action without Russian permission. Mao was contemptuous of Po Ku's subservience to Moscow but himself urged caution in dealing with the rebels until their exact motives could be ascertained. None of the generals involved had ever shown leftist leanings previously and Mao did not trust them.

The Comintern sent word to cooperate with the rebels in fighting the common enemy but to avoid any political agreement with them. From this point on, the Communist Party's actions in regard to the Fukien revolt is completely confused. On one hand, Mao is pictured as urging caution in dealing with the rebels. This is countered by Mao's statement to Edgar Snow in 1936 that "we could have successfully cooperated with Fukien, but due to the advice of Li Teh . . . we withdrew instead."

Curiously, when the Central Committee deposed Mao and placed him under arrest, one of the charges lodged against him was that he hindered rapport between the Party and the Fukien rebels. This, the charges read, prevented the Central Committee from taking proper advantage of the situation.

Regardless of whose fault it was, the Communist Party's

failure to aid the Fukien rebels caused the Fukien revolt to collapse in January, 1934. The revolt was crushed by Chiang Kai-shek while the quarreling Communist Party was holding its Second All-China Soviet Congress. The delegates reelected Mao chairman of the Kiangsi soviet government, but that was an empty gesture, taken solely to keep from alienating the local peasants who still supported Mao. In actuality, the republic government was in the hands of Chang Wen-tien with Mao as a figurehead. Of all the former Maoists only Chu Teh retained a seat on the Central Committee.

The next few months are a complete blank in Mao Tse-tung's life. We can assume that he did not take his downgrading lightly. His past history indicates that he used his powers of logic and persuasion to build support for himself against his political enemies.

Both Kung Chu (in *The Red Army and I*) and Chang Kuo-tao, an old Mao enemy, claim that the bitter fight between the Bolsheviks and the Maoists ended with Mao's being excluded from party meetings and placed under house arrest in Yutu, sixty miles west of Juichin, the soviet capital. He was guarded by the notorious Teng Fa, who headed the secret political police organized by Po Ku.

Mao's arrest was ordered by the Comintern in Moscow and was arranged by Po Ku through his friend Wang Ming, who still worked for Pavel Mif. The reason for the decision to arrest Mao is obscure. The only solid fact regarding it comes from an offhand remark made by a former Communist who became a refugee in Hong Kong. He said, "Oh, everybody knows Mao was arrested because he tried to take advantage of Kuangchang."

From this statement, we can start digging. Kuangchang was the single most disastrous battle fought during any of the five Extermination Campaigns. Li Teh decided that Kuangchang on the Kiangsi-Fukien border was the weakest sector in the Kuomintang encirclement that contained the Communist army. He insisted on attacking it with the full force of the Red

Army. Mao argued against it. He insisted that the Red Army should be broken into guerrilla units. Each should find its way out of the blockade as best it could, and then they could recombine at some later point.

Li Teh brushed aside Mao's suggestion. According to a witness, the German pounded the table with his fist and arrogantly told Mao that he knew nothing about warfare. The Chinese generals seemed awed by the German militarist. Again they sided with Li Teh against Mao. Mao turned to Chu Teh, who again refused to support his old comrade-in-arms. Chu Teh was already on record as saying that Mao's type of guerrilla warfare would not work against Chiang Kai-shek's blockhouse encirclement.

Frustrated, Mao sat back gloomily while the Red Army took a crushing defeat. Four thousand Communist troops were slain and twenty thousand more were wounded. While Communist sources have claimed that morale stayed high in the Kiangsi soviet to the end, the fact is that morale deteriorated drastically after the Kuangchang defeat. Desertions rose alarmingly. The Red Army was disintegrating.

Mao grabbed the opportunity to strike at Po Ku and Li Teh. He began cornering top army officers, attempting to convince them that the policies of the Central Committee and the military strategy of Li Teh were leading the Communist Party to destruction.

This was a direct challenge to the party leadership and its Moscow affiliations, and it could not be ignored. Li Teh demanded that Mao be silenced. Po Ku, as usual, feared to take any decisive action without Comintern approval. With Pavel Mif, a Mao hater, in charge of the Comintern's Far East Section, approval was a foregone conclusion. Teng Fa, it is said, came in person with a company of his political police to inform Mao that the Central Committee had removed him from all participation in the government.

Mao still retained his title as Chairman of the Kiangsi Soviet but now totally without power. Teng Fa moved Mao to Yutu, where Mao was restricted to his house by police guards. In two years, Mao had fallen from undisputed leader of a republic of eighteen million people to a rejected prisoner. His entire life had been a series of disasters from which he had always recovered, but his fortunes had never sunk to such a low point. Po Ku, with great satisfaction, announced to his confederates that Mao Tse-tung was through.

There is a story that Chu Teh replied, "Comrade Mao is like the sun: he may set in the evening, but he is up and shining in the morning." It is significant that only Chou En-lai of all those in power failed to disagree with Chu Teh. That made three who believed that Mao was not through, for the prisoner himself was already making plans for his comeback.

Mao was certain that Li Teh's strategy would lead to military disaster. He was sure the Red Army would collapse as a unit. Then its only chance to survive would be to break into guerrilla units and fade into the mountains. This was Mao's type of fighting. Only Chu Teh surpassed him at it. Under such conditions, Mao was certain that the Bolshevik leadership would collapse. The party would have to turn back to Mao Tse-tung for the leadership needed to prevent its total destruction.

In later years Mao showed his feelings toward his party's leaders during this period. As quoted by John E. Rue, Mao wrote: "Instead of regarding the veteran cadres [i.e. the Maoists] as valuable assets to the party, the sectarians [the Bolsheviks] persecuted, punished and deposed large numbers of these veterans in central and local organizations . . . . large numbers of good comrades were wrongly indicted and unjustly punished; this led to the most lamentable losses inside the party."

In another passage, Mao accused Po Ku's clique of violating "the fundamental principle of democratic centralism," and said that they "eliminated the democratic spirit of criticism and self-criticism, turned party discipline into mechanical regulation, fostered tendencies toward blind obedience and parrotry, and thus jeopardized and obstructed the development of vigorous and creative Marxism.''

In that bitter denunciation, Mao Tse-tung was accusing Po Ku of trying to be another Stalin. Under Mao, any member of the soviet had been free to voice his opinions and criticisms up to the point when a final decision was made. His policy had now been replaced with the Stalin method of vigorously stifling all criticism, both inside and outside the ruling clique.

By that time the slowly tightening Kuomintang siege line had squeezed the Kiangsi republic into half its former area. The need for salt had become acute. Ammunition stores had dropped to the critical point. The end was near. The party leaders considered the disastrous situation in a series of emergency strategy meetings. Mao was not permitted to give his views at any of them. However, Chu Teh came down to Yutu to talk to Mao and presented the Maoist viewpoint. Mao still believed the Red Army should break into small guerrilla bands and try to get away. Li Teh argued for a mass breakthrough by the combined army, and his arguments prevailed.

As a test, an army of ten thousand men was picked to make the breakthrough. At the same time, Chu Teh mounted an offensive on the Fukien border. The Kuomintang rushed reinforcements to that sector, for they feared Chu Teh above all the other commanders. This diversion permitted the escaping army to break the blockade with relative ease. The escapees wheeled, then, and headed for northwestern Hunan to join Ho Lung's small soviet above Changsha.

Heartened by this success, the party leaders now planned a mass breakthrough by the rest of the Red Army, which now numbered about 100,000. This did not include the 20,000 wounded in the disastrous Kuangchang battle. They were dispersed to mountain hospital camps. They retained their guns and received orders to join local guerrilla and partisan groups when they recovered.

The evacuation plan, as finally worked out, was not just for a retreat, but for a complete migration. There were 70,000 actual soldiers and 30,000 party officials and porters. The arsenal and uniform factory were dismantled. The pieces were divided among the porters to carry. Mules were packed with spare ammunition, rice and the Mexican silver that comprised much of the party's treasury.

The vanguard and the rear guard carried only their weapons, ammunition, and five pounds of rice slung in a "sausage bag" over their shoulders. They traveled light, for they had to fight at a moment's notice. In the rest of the army, in addition to his own personal equipment, each man had a shoulder pole with which he carried extra supplies.

A veteran left this description of the common soldier: "Each man's pack contained a blanket or quilt, one quilted winter uniform in addition to the summer uniform he wore, and three pairs of strong cloth shoes with thick rope soles. Each man had a drinking cup and a pair of chopsticks, thrust into his puttees. All men wore big sun-rain hats made of bamboo with oiled paper between the two thin layers. Each carried a rifle. Everyone going on the Long March was dressed and equipped the same."

The line of march was split into three columns. The two outside columns were the fighting troops. The center column was composed of the headquarters of the Central Committee, the student brigade, the supply corps, the medical corps and the propaganda department.

In addition to the men, twenty-six women were permitted to go along. They were all wives of top officials. No children were taken except some pre-teen war orphans who had attached themselves to the army as messengers, orderlies and nurses. Mao had to leave his two small children by Ho Tzu-hun with peasants. He never saw them again. There is no record of the whereabouts of his son by Yang Kai-hui during this time.

The evacuation, which turned into the famous Long March, began October 13 with maneuvering to confuse the Red

Army's intentions. The command for the real beginning was given on the night of October 18, 1934. The central column headed toward Yutu, where Mao joined the march, and then moved due west toward the sector chosen for the attempted breakthrough. After confusing maneuvers, the two flank columns fell into place beside the central column. Earlier, Chu Teh had permitted fake documents to fall into the hands of Kuomintang spies, indicating the Red Army's intention of striking again at Kuangchang, to the east. The false information deceived the Kuomintang commanders, and when the Red Army struck, the surprise was complete.

Mao Tse-tung joined the Long March at Yutu. There had been some question about letting him participate at all. Many of his followers had been shunted into the group detailed to remain in Kiangsi. Chu Teh stood up for Mao, insisting that his old comrade in arms be assigned to Chu Teh's First Front Army as political commissar. The Central Committee reluctantly agreed.

For Mao Tse-tung that was a moment of destiny. He never doubted his ability eventually to defeat his enemies within the party, but participation in the Long March would certainly make it easier, for he would be there on the spot when Po Ku and Li Teh made their inevitable mistakes.

9

The Fight at Tsunyi

Colonel Chen Chang-feng was a twenty-year-old soldier in 1934. He was detailed as Mao's orderly. Twenty-three years later he wrote an account of his adventures during the Long March. He told how Mao left Yutu by the North Gate about five o'clock in the evening.

"Soon the sun set and gusts of bitter cold wind chilled us," Colonel Chen wrote. "The Chairman wore a gray cloth uniform, with no great coat. He walked with enormous strides along the river bank."

After several miles of walking, they came to a floating bridge made from barges lashed together. The bridge was jammed with people as they joined the exodus. Before they had gone far, word filtered back that the vanguard of the Red Army had broken through the enemy's first line of defense. Cheered, the marchers lighted torches to guide their way in the dark. Colonel Chen said the line of flickering lights resembled fire-dragons. He added that the marchers' laughter mingled with songs and shouts, echoing along the line.

The laughter was to be of short duration. Breaking the line itself was surprisingly easy. Chu Teh smashed through the first and second line of enemy positions with a concentrated hammer-blow of massed troops. Once they had broken a hole, the Red Army troops who got through then wheeled and attacked the demoralized Kuomintang troops from the rear. The enemy fell back. Before they could rally, the Red Army was through the breach and heading for the hills of Hunan.

What they thought would be the hardest part—breaking the line—had proven the easiest. Now that they were past the blockhouses, where they had expected the rough country to shield them, the going was exceptionally difficult. One of the reasons was that previously Chu Teh's guerrilla troops traveled light in the hills. Now the Red Army was heavily burdened with supplies and slowed by thousands of porters loaded with pieces of machinery.

The large force was difficult to hide by day when Chiang's reconnaissance planes and fighter-bombers sought them out. Reports claimed that the Red Army lost five thousand men during the first ten days of the Long March.

Their hardship mounted as they proceeded. They could not get away from the constant harrassment by Chiang Kai-shek's pursuing troops. Worse yet, they took the same route as that of the previous ten thousand who had escaped into northwestern Hunan to join Ho Lung. This betrayed their intention and future route to Chiang's planners. So while his southern army continued to harrass the fleeing Communists, Chiang massed other troops in Hunan to cut off their advance.

Sometimes during their halts, Chu Teh would join Mao Tse-tung. The two would hold long talks as they discussed their current military problems and the uncertain future before them. Mao was convinced that they would never be able to get across Hunan to join Ho Lung. Chu Teh agreed, but cautioned Mao against trying to buck the Central Committee just then.

During that grueling period they forced-marched for

seventy-two hours, marching four, resting four, and then repeating the cycle, until they reached rough territory where they had better cover.

When their line of march led through timbered country where trees helped to shield them from Chiang's planes, they resumed daytime marching and rested at night.

In the evenings after their rice was boiled and eaten, Mao organized his political corps to keep up his men's spirits. Actors in the army put on revolutionary skits designed to instruct and amuse. They held sing-songs both in the evening rest periods and on the march. All songs had a revolutionary slant or message. There were rousing speeches and denunciations of Chiang Kai-shek and his appeasement of the Japanese.

Once he got his political corps organized, Mao took little part in the day-to-day indoctrination. His orderlies set up a crude table for him at every stop. Here he often worked far into the night on his maps and papers. He wrote a lot, making plans and working out political theories. He carefully noted every mistake—political, tactical or strategical—and worked out the correct solution.

The Red Army took four towns, replenishing their food stores in each, and then came close to disaster crossing the Hsiang River as they moved across the southern tip of Hunan into the northern tip of Kwangsi Province. They captured a pontoon bridge, but Chiang's air force blew it out of the water before all the Red Army could get over. Most of the Communist soldiers came from inland China and had never learned to swim. Hundreds died when the bridge broke, and several regiments were stranded. Unable to swim the flooded river, they broke into small units and joined partisan guerrilla bands in the Hunan hills.

Chinese historians all agree that Hsiang was a major battle. None agree on the number of casualties, however. One places them as high as 50,000, others as low as 5,000. Li Teh, however, claimed that the losses were light from the time the Long March started in Juichin until it reached Tsunyi in

January. Since Li Teh was directing strategy during that time, his claim of light losses is probably an attempt to justify his military tactics.

After crossing the Hsiang River, the Red columns turned back into Hunan to drive north for the reunion with Ho Lung's forces. They ran into a solid wall of Kuomintang troops and had to fall back. The Revolutionary Military Council, headed by Chou En-lai, held a hasty conference. All the generals and top officials attended except Mao Tse-tung, who was not invited. However, both Chu Teh and Peng Teh-huai gave Mao an account of what went on.

Mao listened and said nothing, but that night he again worked late. He covered several pages with notes and suggestions. He also found time to talk earnestly and persuasively to Chu Teh and Peng Teh-huai. Sometime later, he found occasion to talk with Lin Piao and Lo Ping-hui, who each commanded a corps.

The talks had a single purpose—to undermine Li Teh and Chou En-lai as military strategists and Po Ku as Party leader.

The Revolutionary Military Council decided to abandon any further attempt to join Ho Lung. Instead, they made a new plan to move into Kweichow Province, preparatory to cutting across Szechuan Province to join Chang Kuo-tao and Hsu Hsiang-chien, who were supporting a soviet at Pachou near the Szechuan-Shensi border.

Mao received this information with a passive face, but it was a blow to him. There was a chance that the Red Army could fight its way through Kweichow and Szechuan to join Chang Kuo-tao. But if they did, it would defeat Mao's plot to regain control. Chang Kuo-tao and Mao hated each other. Chang would certainly throw all his power to Po Ku and Li Teh in any showdown with Mao.

Also, even putting aside his own personal ambitions, Mao did not believe that the Szechuan soviet could withstand a determined drive by Chiang Kai-shek. If the refugees from Kiangsi joined Chang Kuo-tao, it would, in Mao's opinion, be only a short time before Chang's soviet would be destroyed, just as the Kiangsi soviet had been.

As the only alternative, Mao picked a small Communist soviet in upper Shensi near Inner Mongolia and close to the famous Great Wall of China. There, Mao felt, they could hold their own against Chiang's extermination campaigns. After regaining strength there, the Red Army could move east toward Peking or southeast through Szechuan toward Hunan again. He discussed this only with Chu Teh, who listened but made no comment.

The Red Army now moved east into Kweichow Province. December rains turned their roads into seas of mud, but the weather hampered the enemy as much as it did the Red Army. The factions fought an almost continual battle as they slowly advanced. The fighting finally reached a climax at the Wu River as the refugee army approached Tsunyi. Here they were boxed in by four armies, the Kuomintang's Nationalist Army that had pursued them from Kiangsi, the Hunan Provincial Army, the Szechuan Provincials, and the Kweichow army.

The terrain was exceedingly rough. "To advance a single mile, we had to walk five miles up and down," one general reported. "The land was that hilly." Although this made marching difficult at first, later it was the salvation of the fleeing Red Army. The thousands of gorges, defiles, cliffs and streams provided them cover and avenues of escape when surrounded. Thus by adroit maneuvering most of the Red Army was able to fight its way to the river. There Chu Teh captured a bridge before the defenders could destroy it.

The main part of the army got safely across the river, but General Lo Ping-hui's rearguard corps was cut off as it fought to delay the main mass of the pursuing Kuomintang Army. Lin Piao waited as long as he could, but when it appeared that Szechuan troops were going to break through, Lin blew up the Wu River bridge to prevent the Nationalists from attacking his army. This stranded Lo Ping-hui below the river.

Although trapped and outnumbered fifty to one, Lo

managed to fight his way through the enemy's encirclement and made his own river crossing seventy-five miles below the route taken by the rest of the Red Army.

The Communists took a serious mauling at the Wu. Loss figures from that tough battle are contradictory, running from five to fifteen thousand slain. It could not be called a defeat, since the Reds achieved their objective, but it was one of the costly victories that cut their strength so much that a few more like it would destroy them.

After taking such a hard blow at the Wu River, the Red Army got a break at Tsunyi, a town in north Kweichow. Ten miles from the city, the Red Army's Fourth Regiment captured some high-ranking Kuomintang officers. From them the communist regimental political commissar learned full details of the city's defenses. He then disguised a company of Red soldiers in Kuomintang uniforms. They took along the prisoners who had agreed to assist and marched to Tsunyi's walls in a driving rain, arriving after 11 P.M.

The gate guards at first refused to open to the newcomers. But then the cooperative captives identified themselves and satisfied the guards that this indeed was one of their own companies. The Red Army company marched through the gates, wheeled and put the surprised guards under arrest. To the blare of bugles blowing the "charge," they spread through the city. Within an hour all resistance ended. The main mass of the Red Army marched into Tsunyi the next day.

It was then the first week of January. The Red Army dug in to resist any attempt of the Kuomintang to retake the city. Chiang Kai-shek, however, was not anxious to risk his army against the hastily prepared defenses in Tsunyi. His spies had already reported that the Red Army's real objective was Chungking, across the Yangtze River in Szechuan Province. So while the Red Army rested in Tsunyi, Chiang began massing his troops to annihilate them when they attempted to cross the Yangtze.

Mao was greatly disturbed when he learned that Po Ku and

Li Teh had decided to attack Chungking. This was a direct return to Li Li-sanism with its emphasis on attacking the big cities. Mao was convinced that such a tactic was suicide. The information he got from the secret talks in the Central Committee was that Po Ku and Li Teh had abandoned their earlier announced plan to team up with Chang Kuo-tao's soviet in north Szechuan. Instead, they hoped to hold the city of Chungking, organize the industrial workers there, and establish a Russian-type proletariat revolutionary group.

Such a move, Mao felt, would be exactly like the earlier attack on Changsha. They might win the city, but the proletariat base was too small to support a soviet state. They would eventually be destroyed and forced to flee again. Once again the Central Committee was giving in to the Comintern, who seemed unable to understand that Russian communism had to be modified to be successful in China.

Mao now moved swiftly, with the confidence he always felt in himself. He was sure Lin Piao was on his side. Chu Teh, who had sided against Mao in the previous showdown, now was disenchanted with Li Teh's military direction. Mao knew he could count on his old comrade-in-arms in this crisis, although Chu Teh had an annoying way of making up his own mind at times that clashed with Mao's objectives. Mao next brought his strong powers of persuasion to bear on Peng Teh-huai and received his promise of support. He also talked with Chung Teng-hang, another Corps commander.

With this solid military support behind him, Mao directly challenged Po Ku and Li Teh. He demanded a meeting of an "enlarged" Central Committee. The "enlargement" meant that he and the military commanders would sit in on the meeting. Previously only Chu Teh had been a member of the Committee. Po Ku refused, coldly telling Mao that the Committee had met at Li-ping a few weeks before and another meeting was not required.

Mao pointed out that the Chinese Communist Party was supposed to be a democratic organization. If it had ceased to

be, then force would be in order. Po Ku got the point. He
hastily conferred with Li Teh and Chou En-lai. Li Teh tried to
threaten Mao with reprisals by the Comintern for his high-
handed manner, but Mao replied that they were far from
Russia, surrounded by the enemy, and in danger of annihi-
lation. In his opinion the Comintern could neither help nor
hurt him. Chou En-lai, surprising Po Ku, declared himself in
favor of the meeting.

None of the participants in the meeting chose to discuss it
much, later. From what information has come out, it appears
that Po Ku opened the meeting with a spirited defense of his
decisions and the military strategy employed. (Emi Siao
claimed that Mao opened the meeting with a denunciation of
Po Ku.) Po was followed by Mao Tse-tung. Mao spoke from
notes amassed during his long evenings' work. He began with
the Fukien rebellion, claiming that Po Ku and the Central
Committee had lost the Kiangsi soviet because of their failure
to make common cause with the rebels. He denounced the
choice of route out of Kiangsi, which he claimed had tele-
graphed their intentions to Chiang Kai-shek's commanders.
He went on to denounce the lack of democracy and attention
to minority members of the Party, and the failure properly to
indoctrinate many of the troops, which had led to poor
morale.

Almost to a man Chinese writers have insisted that army
morale was always high during the Long March. Lo Ping-hui,
who commanded the IX Army Corps rearguard, is one of the
few who admitted otherwise. He said moral was indeed bad
during this period. Desertions were higher than at any time
since the Autumn Harvest Uprising.

Mao also denounced the poor military strategy and tactics
of Li Teh, but he did not dwell upon that point. Chu Teh,
who followed Mao in the order of speakers, made devastating
accusations against the competency of the Revolutionary
Military Council. The RMC was headed by Chou En-lai, although Li Teh actually formulated policy. Peng Teh-huai

followed Chu Teh with additional complaints about the military decisions made since they left Kiangsi.

Li Teh defended his policies and insisted that they were supported by the Comintern. Since Li Teh could not speak Chinese, his angry defense of himself was translated by Po Ku. The German went on to hint that any obstruction of his policies would bring retailiation by the Russians. Again Mao contemptuously brushed aside any question of Russian displeasure. He had been displeasing Stalin since 1927.

Chou En-lai was the next speaker. He electrified the assembly by readily acknowledging that he and the Central Committee had made some great mistakes. Po Ku was stunned. He owed his position as Party chief to the combined support of the Twenty-Eight Bolsheviks, of which he was a member, and the Whampoa Clique, led by Chou En-Lai. Po Ku knew that if Chou deserted him he lacked the votes to remain in power.

The arguments continued, sometimes getting so loud that they could be heard by the soldiers in the assembly hall courtyard. The meeting was held in the top floor of a two-story palace owned as a summer home by the governor of Kweichow. Then the turning point came when Chou En-lai suddenly proposed that Po Ku resign and that the assembly replace him with Mao Tse-tung. The motion was put to a vote and carried.

Mao's victory was assured by the support of the generals. Just why Chou En-lai decided to abandon Po Ku is not clear. The Twenty-Eight Bolsheviks were not convinced that Mao could get them out of their difficulties. In fact, Li Teh allegedly advised Po Ku not to fight Mao's takeover, because the Maoists would fail and the former directors could move easily back into command. Chou apparently did not agree with this view and preferred to throw his lot with Mao Tse-tung.

With the fall of Po Ku, Mao became Chairman of the Central Committee, with the Bolshevik Chang Wen-tien as

Secretary-General. Chang's taking the second spot below Mao is curious. He had always been opposed to Mao and had voted to expell Mao from the Party at one time. The military setup remained the same, except that Li Teh was removed from all policy-making and Chou En-lai resigned from the Revolutionary Military Council but kept a position on the Central Committee.

While the Red Army was resting in Tsunyi, Chiang Kai-shek was massing both Kuomintang and provincial troops in another encirclement movement. There was some fighting as Red Army units probed toward the Yangtze, but for the most part fighting was light as the Kuomintang developed positions for the coming knockout blow.

Finally, in the last week of January, the full forces of the Red Army attempted to fight their way across the Yangtze River, but met such resistance that they had to retreat to Tsunyi again. In the meantime, Kuomintang troops had defeated Chang Kuo-tao's Fourth Front Army in north Szechuan. Chang retreated toward the Tibetan border. Politically, Chang's retreat aided Mao, since it had been Po Ku's plan to join with Chang's small soviet. His failure helped to prove Mao right. At this point Mao had already decided that their only hope lay in getting to Shensi province. He made that decision soon after the decisions in Hunan showed that they would never be able to join Ho Lung in north Hunan.

But although he intended to take the Long March due North, Mao split his army and headed south. He sent Lin Piao's I Corps in the direction of Kunming (Yunnanfu), capital of Yunnan Province. Then he set the rest of the First Front Army maneuvering north of Kunming. He tried to give the impression that the Communists' intentions were to capture Kunming with the intention of setting up a soviet there.

Such a maneuver was logical. Under its former directors the Chinese Communist Party had concentrated on industrialized urban centers. In addition, Yunnan was the home province of both Chu Teh and Lo Ping-hui. They had many supporters there. It was good reasoning to assume that the Red Army would try to make its base there.

Chiang now frantically shifted his armies, weakening his northern line to rush reinforcements south. But instead of attacking Kunming as Chiang expected, Lin Piao wheeled at the very gates of that city and rushed north to join the rest of the Red Army. They captured boats by a ruse and crossed the Yangtze into Szechuan.

It was then March. They had been on the Long March for six months. Losses in battle and by desertions were about fifty percent. Part of the manpower loss was made up by recruiting peasants and Kuomintang deserters. Deserter-recruits were not put into battle until they had undergone extensive political indoctrination. No opportunity was lost to increase the soldiers' hatred of Chiang Kai-shek and his Nationalist government, or to make each soldier feel a part of the movement to save China. Since the majority of the troops were of peasant stock, the propaganda emphasized the oppression of the farming class, picturing Mao Tse-tung and the Red Army as their champions.

Surprisingly, although the Red Army has suffered a fifty percent loss of personnel and was handicapped by many wounded, morale improved considerably after Tsunyi. Mao succeeded in reestablishing a sense of purpose among the men. Morale, even more incredibly, stayed high although they faced some of the worst conditions any fighting force ever endured as they progressed.

After crossing the Yangtze, known here as the Golden Sands River, Mao headed north. The army paralleled the Tibetan border, plunging into a land few Chinese had ever ventured into. It was an area wild beyond belief, peopled by aborigine tribes who passionately hated the Chinese. The Red Army, weakened by fatigue, sickness and starvation, faced bitter battles with those natives as well as a constant pounding by Chiang Kai-shek's bombers.

During one of the bombing raids, Mao's pregnant wife was

struck by bomb fragments and had to be carried in a litter. Mao's fever had returned. He was gaunt and barely able to cling to his saddle as his Tibetan pony picked its way along the rocky mountain trails the army was following.

Such trails were hard climbing, but they were welcome, for the army knew by previous experience that the narrow defiles would keep away the bombing and strafing planes of the enemy. By that time most of the excess equipment Po Ku had brought from Kiangsi had long since been lost or abandoned. Chu Teh refused to part with the sewing machines. They were still carried on the backs of porters. Also, Mao Tse-tung had insisted on keeping a small flat-bed press and fonts of type. Any time the army had a rest of any length of time, brief newspapers and propaganda posters were printed on whatever paper could be secured in captured towns. The army had some captured radios and kept in touch with world events in that way. Thus Mao was able to make use of news about continued Japanese aggressions against China in his Party propaganda for his army.

After leaving the Yangtze River crossing, the Red Army plunged into what is called the "big bend" country. There the Yangtze, which has been flowing south through deep gorges along the Tibetan frontier, suddenly bends due east and then north before taking another bend to head northeast past Chungking and Wuhan to empty finally into the South China Sea at Shanghai. This bend country in Szechuan is peopled by aborigine tribes who call themselves *I-min* and are known as Lolos by the Chinese.

The Lolos were one of the few aborigine tribes that the invading Hans (Chinese) had been unable to displace when the Hans moved from Chinese Turkestan into what is now China some 4,000 years ago. The wild nature of their mountains and their savage fighting ability preserved the Lolos' independence to modern times. Their territory covered 11,000 square miles. Mao and Chu Teh knew that the Lolos would be more formidable an enemy than the low-morale Kuomintang troops or the opium-sodden Szechuan provincial army. However, they had no choice but to plunge directly into Lololand. If they tried to go around it, they would run head-on into the mass of Kuomintang troops at Chengtu where they would be suffocated by sheer numbers. If they tried to swing west around Lololand, they would find themselves in the highlands of Tibet, where equally fierce hillmen and adverse climate would destroy them.

10
Death March

The first fight between the First Front Army and the Lolos came in a deserted village on the edge of Lololand. The Chinese who inhabited the village fled at the approach of the Red Army. The Lolos, intent on plunder, descended on the village at the same time the Red Army marched in.

Mao had given strict orders to avoid conflict with the aborigines if at all possible. He hoped to win them to his side as he had won the peasants of the areas they had passed through. However, the Red vanguard had no alternative except to fight or be destroyed. They beat back the aborigines and managed to capture several.

Mao ordered his political corps to go to work on the captives and try to convince them that the Red Army was their friend. He did not have much hope that they would succeed. Beating down age-old animosities would take time. The Red Army could not afford to wait.

Then Mao got an unexpected break. He learned that one of

his officers, Liu Pei-cheng, had formerly been a *min-tuan*, or private army officer, in Szechuan and had often fought the Lolos. Mao and Chu Teh closely questioned Liu about their new enemy. Mao was still sick. He sat staring dully ahead while Chu Teh questioned the officer. Only when Liu mentioned that the Lolos were divided into two groups, a "Black Lolo" clan and a "White Lolo" clan, did Mao come to life. He rubbed his burning face and turned to look at Chu Teh. The general also hunched forward eagerly. His eyes gleamed as Liu went on to say that the Black Lolos were the dominant group and made slaves of the White Lolos.

Any place where groups are in conflict is fertile ground for the Communist divide-and-conquer tactic. Despite his illness, Mao personally talked to the highest-ranking officer among the prisoners. The man could talk Chinese, and when they ran into language difficulties, Liu, who could speak the Lolo dialect, interpreted for them.

The Lolos had been prepared for their audience with Mao by extremely courteous and friendly treatment by their captors. This bewildered the prisoners, who were prepared to be executed. Then Mao, drawing upon the information he had received from Liu, explained that there were Red and White Chinese just as there were Black Lolos and White Lolos in their land. Also, that the two Chinese groups were enemies just as the Lolos were.

Mao went on to explain that the Chinese who had fought and mistreated the Lolos for so many years were the White Chinese. The Reds wanted to be their friends and help them fight the Whites. After that speech had time to sink in, Mao ordered the prisoners released and sent Liu back with them to their tribe. The gratitude of the prisoners was sincere. They interceded with the tribal chief for the Reds. He in turn made Liu his blood-brother and promised the Red Army safe conduct through his territory.

Unfortunately, there is no central government among the Lolos. The tribes are independent. That chief's safe conduct applied only to his jurisdiction. However, he sent along Lolos to accompany the Reds on their march through Lololand and they negotiated for Mao with each successive tribe. This help permitted the Red Army to move through Lololand without war, but it did not prevent worrisome troubles.

Hse Meng-chui, the Red Army historian, told Nym Wales that the Lolos were first-class thieves. "The tribesmen were never satisfied and took more and more. They looked in the pockets of our soldiers . . . In fact they took everything portable."

Only the strict Red Army discipline prevented the often-angry soldiers from shooting the predatory Lolos. This would have been disastrous, for they were then deep in Lololand and surrounded by the aborigines. They moved along smartly, but even so it took three weeks to get through the rough terrain. The heavy timber shielded them from Chiang Kai-shek's reconnaissance planes. The enemy had no idea where they were. Nor did the Kuomintang generals suspect that Mao would be able to make peace with the aborigines. They expected Mao's group to emerge—if the Red Army got through at all—as a badly mauled remnant of an army that they could easily dispatch.

So it was a complete surprise when the full force of the Red Army suddenly burst out of the timber and attacked a large group of Szechuan provincial troops. There was no fight. The provincials surrendered, and the Red Army won badly needed rice stores and munitions.

Mao paused there only long enough to hold peasant meetings to build up partisan support for the Red Army. All extra rice that the Red Army could not carry with it was distributed to the poor peasants. Land deeds were burned and trials were held for cruel landowners and military officers who were accused by the peasants of undue oppression. All were convicted by Mao's courts upon evidence of the peasants. Then the convicted men were turned over to the peasants for punishment. All were executed.

As soon as that operation was accomplished, the Red Army headed north toward Anshunchang where there was a ferry across the Tatu River. The Tatu River crossing appeared to be the climax of their long retreat, for Chiang Kai-shek had moved his headquarters to Cheng-tu, preparing for the next major showdown at the crossing. Anshunchang had now become a symbol to both the Red Army and the Kuomintang. The reason was that Anshunchang was the place where the Manchu government had finally destroyed the Taiping Army in the famous rebellion of the nineteenth century.

That rebellion came close to succeeding but fell apart at the end. Prince Shih Ta-kai had led the defeated rebels in a long march much like the retreat of the defeated Kiangsi army that Mao Tse-tung and Chu Teh were now leading. The Taipings were unable to cross the Tatu River at Anshunchang.

The Tatu River is short but exceedingly deep and wild, since it rises in Sikang and tumbles through fantastically steep gorges on its way to join the Min River and then the Yangtze. The watershed in the spring is tremendous, and the Red Army was arriving in May, when the river is always at flood stage.

Mao, Chu Teh and Chiang Kai-shek, all students of the Taiping Rebellion, knew that the Tatu River crossing was the single most crucial point in the Red Army's long retreat. Chiang, on his part, was determined to repeat the Taiping Massacre that had ended the old rebellion. He sent a personal message to his Szechuan troops urging them to make history repeat itself.

Mao's problem was to avoid the mistakes of the Taipings, otherwise he could expect the Red Army to be destroyed. As for himself and the other leaders, they knew what had happened to Prince Shih when he had fallen into government hands. He was taken back to Cheng-tu. The Viceroy of Szechuan said in his memoirs that Shih was executed there by "the slicing method." This is the horrible torture death that adventure writers of a by-gone age called "The Death of a Thousand Cuts."

Chu Teh, always optimistic, was confident that the Red Army could fight its way to a crossing. The point near Anshunchang was normally guarded by a company or two of Szechuan provincials. The Red Army's unexpectedly rapid traversal of Lololand had put it on the road before Chiang expected it. Chu was confident that they could get to the ferry before Chiang could rush in reinforcements.

They were successful in reaching the Tatu River first. Lin Piao's vanguard I Corps captured three ferry boats and got enough men across the river to surprise the Szechuan garrison there. The river current was so swift and the boats so small that it took four days to ferry I Corps across the Tatu. In the meantime, the main body of the Red Army arrived and had to make camp to await their time to cross.

Disaster struck on the afternoon of the fourth day. As the last of I Corps was on the boats, Chiang Kai-shek's airplanes found the Red Army. The first pass destroyed one ferry at the dock and sank the other two in midstream. About eighty soldiers drowned. The Red Army was now split by the rampaging river. Lin Piao could not return and the main body of the army could not join him.

There was an immediate conference to consider what they could do in the face of this calamity. It had been an inability to cross the Tatu to escape from a better armed and larger force that destroyed the Taipings. The Red Army now faced a similar disaster. Po Ku and Li Teh offered no suggestions. They wanted no part of the blame when the Red Army was destroyed. It all belonged to Mao Tse-tung.

The logical course would have been to disband the Red Army, break it into small, individual guerrilla units and let each take its own way in trying to break through the enemy forces closing in upon them. Mao, however, was not yet ready for that drastic maneuver. While it might save a lot of lives, it would set back the Communist cause by years and maybe decades, for it would be difficult to bring all the small units back together into a strong fighting force.

Instead, he ordered a march upriver to Lutingchiao where an iron-chain bridge had been built in 1701. No one was sure of the present condition of the bridge or knew how well it was guarded. One thing was sure, Lutingchiao was the end of the line. If they failed to make the crossing there, they had no choice but to disband and try to get away in small groups.

They signaled their intention to Lin Piao on the opposite bank. Then both groups set out on a forced march up the banks of the rampaging river toward the village of Lutingchiao, about ninety miles upstream. For a while they could see each other. Then the mountains cut off their view and also interferred with radio reception.

At one point, unknown to Mao's group, Lin Piao became involved in a fight and had to detour. That delay permitted a Szechuan Provincial group to get ahead of them. Chu Teh did not discover it until a narrowing of the river brought the bank trails close together again. He called for double time and shorter rest periods, pushing his exhausted troops to the limit in an attempt to get to Lutingchiao before the Szechuan troops could destroy the bridge.

The ancient bridge was made by attaching nine huge chains in concrete and stretching them across the river. The hand-forged links of the chains were as large as rice bowls. Planks had been laid across these nine lines. Four extra chains, two on each side, served as hand rails and for support. An arched gate stood at each end of the 300-yard span.

The Red Army won the race to the bridge but found that the garrison in Luting, the village across the river, had removed the planks from the two-thirds of the bridge on the south side. Also, a machine gun position and riflemen were zeroed in on the chains. There were still less than fifty of the defenders, but at any moment they would be reinforced by the Szechuan Provincials the Red Army had been racing along the river banks. Somewhere behind the Provincials was Lin Piao, but no one knew how far back his corps was.

Chu Teh looked at the naked chains on their side of the river.

"Call for volunteers," he said.

All within the sound of his voice volunteered before the order could be passed on. A platoon commander named Ma Ta-chiu was selected. He in turn went through several companies picking the strongest men he could find. Most of his own platoon were too weak from fatigue and starvation. Also, while he wanted strong men, he did not want big men, for their weight would be a handicap in swinging across the bridge.

While Ma Ta-chiu picked his men, infantry troops lined the banks of the river to divert the enemy's attention from the men who would try to cross the chains. Others were set to chopping logs to replace the planks if the crossing was successful.

When Ma signaled that he was ready, the infantry cut loose with machine gun and rifle fire. Ma's men, armed only with pistols, hand grenades and long knives, slipped around the concrete buttresses that anchored the bridge chains. Each man in turn grasped the chain links and began swinging across. The chains jerked and swayed under their weight. They had to move swiftly to avoid presenting too stable a target, but at the same time they had to be careful to grasp each link just right to keep from getting their fingers crushed as the links ground together.

The river narrowed at that point, which was why the bridge had been constructed there. The water, imprisoned between the high rock walls, churned and splashed in fury. No one who dropped into it could hope to swim. It was sure death to fall.

They had swung only a few feet along the chains when the Szechuan defenders on the other side spotted them. Machine gun muzzles swung their way, and a deadly hail of bullets raked across the chains. Frantic Red gunners fired back at the muzzle blasts of the enemy.

Mao Tse-tung and Chu Teh watched the desperate fight from a high elevation. Neither spoke, but both knew that their fate and the fate of their revolution was being decided by the heroic twenty men swinging monkey-fashion across the chains.

The enemy machine guns were forced to fire at an acute angle. Although that caused many of the bullets to glance off the huge iron links, the protection was not enough. Five of Ma's men were knocked off the chains by enemy fire before they had swung ten feet. Within another two minutes five more had died. Chu Teh, watching grim-faced beside the silent Mao Tse-tung, signaled for another squad to get ready.

Just as Mao and Chu Teh were deciding that Ma's men could not get across, the Szechuan commander drew an opposite conclusion. He had removed only two-thirds of the planks from the bridge chains, thinking that would be sufficient to stop the Reds. Now it appeared to him that some of Ma's soldiers might get that far after all.

He bawled a loud command. Obediently three of his soldiers grabbed cans of kerosene and rushed out to douse the oil on the remaining planks. Red Army machine gunners cut down on them with bursts of bullets. Ma, the platoon leader, tried to swing up on the planks as the Szechuan soldiers set the oil afire. A rifle bullet knocked him into the churning water. Others tried to follow and died with Ma.

Then one man, identified only as the platoon political advisor, managed to get off the chains onto the burning boards. He was screened from the gunners' view by the fire and smoke. He jerked the pins on his hand grenades and sprang through the wall of flame. He managed to hurl the grenades just as a spray of machine gun fire cut his body in half.

The grenade struck the machine gun nest. The three remaining members of the original twenty rushed forward, hurling their own grenades. The defenders fell back in confusion. More Red soldiers began swinging across the chains, as still others rushed logs down to replace the missing planks.

As they rushed across the hastily repaired bridge, the extra Szechuan troops the Red Army had raced down the river now arrived. The battle increased in fury and then broke suddenly when Lin Piao arrived with the rest of the Red Army. The Nationalist Chinese troops broke and fled.

The remainder of the Red Army quickly crossed the river and began a forced march into the hills. Here they paused only long enough to hold a memorial ceremony for the seventeen men killed in the initial storming of the bridge.

Earlier, Chang Kuo-tao had been routed from his soviet in eastern Szechuan and had retreated to Moukung, which was a hundred miles directly north of Mao's position at Lutingchiao and the Tatu River bridge. Mao's plan now called for proceeding to Moukung, combining with Chang's Fourth Front Army, and then marching with the strengthened force to Yenan, where Mao felt they would be safe. His plan differed from Po Ku's original suggestion that they join Chang Kuo-tao. Chang operated a soviet, and Po Ku's plan had called for them to make a settlement there with him. Now, since Chang had been driven from his original location, Mao called for Chang Kuo-tao to join them in the march morth. Chang and Mao were enemies, but it had always been Mao's policy to bring his enemies into his fold whenever possible.

Chu Teh estimated that they could cover the hundred miles in two and a half days under normal forced marching conditions. They had often averaged forty miles a day. However, the high, glacial mountains they faced would slow their progress. Even so, Chu Teh told Mao, they should complete the march within a week or ten days. Actually, the journey took two months and an appalling death toll.

Their first obstacle was a vicious battle with Tibetan cavalry hired by the Kuomintang to attack them. Chu Teh lost five hundred men in the fight but gained considerable stores, ponies, and silver bullion, which Chiang Kai-shek had given the Tibetans in payment.

They struggled through a wet and foggy mountain area where the humid air from subtropic Szechuan met the frigid air from the snow-covered mountains along the Tibetan border. Marching was so difficult through the deep mud and constant rain that Chu Teh was forced to permit a four-day rest before they began climbing into the eternal ice of "Old Snow Mountain."

There they died by the hundreds. Pack animals, unable to keep their feet on the icy trails, plunged over cliffs. More than half were lost. Ill-clad, wet, freezing men crouched to rest and were never able to get up again. But bad as their situation was in the lower levels, it got worse as they climbed higher. They had, for the most part, all come from low altitudes, so they had difficulty breathing in the thin air above 10,000 feet. Then, as they climbed higher, many suffered from mountain sickness. Overcome by nausea and gasping for breath, they fell by the scores and froze where they lay. A doctor who made the march said later that mountain sickness was the direct cause of more deaths than any other single thing during the entire March.

When they reached a valley, the marchers would rest, wet and miserable, until they regained sufficient strength to force their way up the freezing trails of the next mountain. Mao was half dead, scarcely able to sit his saddle as an aide led his horse. Only Chu Teh was immune from the sicknesses and exhaustion that sapped the strength of his companions.

It was July, 1935, when the exhausted, depleted Red Army came out of the mountains, and two weeks later they made contact with Chang Kuo-tao's Fourth Front Red Army. It was a joyous reunion for the soldiers, but Mao Tse-tung received a cold welcome from Chang.

Chang resented Mao's elevation to Party head. He also was conscious of the fact that he had 50,000 fresh troops under his command, while Mao had only slightly over 40,000 exhausted soldiers. In addition, many of Mao's troops were recruits they had picked up along the route and were not trained, seasoned soldiers. Mao, in turn, was displeased to see that Chang Kuo-tao' ruled his soviet as a warlord would, providing special privileges for himself and his officers. The practice was directly contrary to Mao's ideas for a democratic army. However, Mao did not protest either about Chang's uncommunistic attitude toward his army or Chang's discourtesy in not coming immediately to see Mao, as protocol demanded.

Mindful, perhaps, that Chang's fresh army could easily defeat his own, Mao did not challenge Chang directly. Instead, Mao called a special session of the Central Committee to make plans for the future. Having dominated the Central Committee since the big change at Tsunyi, Mao felt confident that he could force Chang to accept his views. He did not feel that Chang Kuo-tao could afford to resist the entire Central Committee.

The plan Mao presented at the meeting called for the First Front Army and the Fourth Front Army to combine. Together they would march on to Shensi to combine with the small soviet there. The combined Red Army would be strong enough to push the Nationalists out of Southern Shensi, providing a haven where the Communist Party could regain its strength before resuming the attack against Chiang Kai-shek.

Chang Kuo-tao was bitterly against combining his army with Mao's and going to Shensi, for it would subordinate him to Mao. The arguments in the Committee became heated and almost violent. When the majority of the Committee sided with Mao, Chang reluctantly agreed to make the march. He did, however, refuse to assimilate his army with the First Front Army. When the march resumed after nearly a month of rest, Chang's Fourth Front Army marched as a separate group several miles to the east of Mao and Chu Teh's First Front Army.

Chang was irritable during the first week of the march. Then he suddenly moved farther away from the First Front Army, a maneuver his chief of staff told Mao was necessary to avoid a battle with a Kuomintang group. This maneuver brought the Fourth Front Army in late August (1935) to a flooded river which Chang declared was unfordable, preventing him from rejoining the Mao legions. He then announced that under the circumstances he had no alternative except to return to his previous location in Szechuan.

At the same time Chang made this announcement, he sent a company of his troops to arrest Chu Teh. Chu Teh, with two corps of the First Front Army, had just come to aid Chang in an expected battle with Kuomintang troops approaching their flank.

That action has never been satisfactorily explained. Edgar Snow, in his famous book, *Red Star Over China*, written after interviews with Mao in Shensi, says only, "There were other factors of intra-party struggle involved which here need not be discussed." The official story is that Chang took Chu Teh prisoner and forced the commander-in-chief to return to Szechuan with him.

But this overlooks the fact that Chu Teh had two corps backing him up and all the rest of the First Front Army if he wanted them. The entire story of the rise of Communist China is the story of former friends turning against each other. The likely explanation is that Chu Teh was disenchanted with Mao's Shensi plan. He was a man of action and Chang's plan to fight for the Szechuan soviet probably appealed to him. Also, Chu Teh may have decided that Mao's days were numbered as the party leader. He knew that Li Te and Po Ku were only waiting for Mao to make a mistake.

In any event, logic dictates that Chu Teh went willingly with Chang. If he had been a prisoner, he would hardly have been permitted to direct Chang's army while Chang devoted himself to the political side.

The loss of Chu Teh was a serious blow to Mao Tse-tung. The two had been so close that they had been considered a single man for nearly seven years. While Mao's political genius had laid the foundation for their successes, it had been Chu Teh's military genius that provided the power base from which Mao could build.

Outwardly Mao seemed unconcerned at his old friend's defection. He moved Peng Teh-huai into the commander's position and resumed the march to Shensi as if nothing had happened. He had no words of blame for either Chang Kuo-tao or for Chu Teh. He said only, "They will join us later."

Mao's one characteristic that seems to have been lacking in all other great leaders was the ability to forgive his enemies. While he was a fierce, bitter fighter and could strike ruthlessly and bloodily—as in the Kiangsi mutiny—when he had to, he preferred to absorb his enemies when he could, bringing them into the Communist fold.

If it had been Stalin, instead of Mao, who had emerged as the victor at Tsunyi, all those who had opposed him would have been shot. Mao preferred to work with his opponents in the interests of party harmony, bringing them eventually to his side with persuasion and logic.

At that point, things looked bleak for Mao. He had lost his strongest supporter and a good many of his soldiers. In addition to the troops that accompanied Chu Teh, Lo Ping-hui had also been cut off and had joined Chang Kuo-tao and Chu Teh. In his own group, Mao faced Po Ku and Li Te, who were waiting for an opportunity to overthrow him. In addition they were headed directly into Mantzu Land, which was peopled by fierce aborigines who hated the Chinese. On top of all this, Mao himself was still ill and weak.

11
The Road to Peking

The shattered remnants of what had once been a great Red army moved cautiously into Mantzu Land. Mao hoped to win their respect as he had won the Lolos' but was unable to make any kind of friendly contact. The same was true with the Hsifan-Tibetans, who occupied the territory beyond Mantzu Land. Both aborigine groups employed guerrilla tactics against the advancing Red Army.

That left Mao in the same position Chiang Kai-shek had been during the Red Army guerrilla attacks. Both were in unfriendly territory and were forced to keep together, while the enemy could break into small groups, strike hard, and then fade back into the forests and mountains. The only way Mao could pursue so many attacking groups would have been to break his own forces into small units. These then would have been at the mercy of vengeful farmers and would have been destroyed. All Mao could do was hold his force together, fight off the repeated attacks, and rush through the aborigines' territory as quickly as he could.

In the beginning, when the terrain was flat, the Mantzus rode out of the hills on their small Tibetan ponies to attack like American Indians routing a wagon train, but after the Red Army passed into the mountains where horses were a handicap, the Mantzus loosened landslides, rolled rocks down on them, and destroyed bridges, causing many Red soldiers to drown. There were no large pitched battles, but the constant attrition caused a greater loss in Red personnel than the army had suffered in any one battle with Chiang Kai-shek's Nationalists.

It took ten days to cross the aborigine territory. This did not alleviate the Red Army's suffering, however, for they now entered the weird "Great Grasslands." Here the enemy was nature rather than man.

The Grasslands was a vast swamp covered with a sea of thick grass. Agnes Smedley described it. "As far as the eye could reach, day after day, the Red Army saw nothing but an endless ocean of high wild grass growing in an icy swamp of black muck and water many feet deep . . . . No tree or shrub grew here, no bird ventured near, no insect sounded. There was nothing, nothing but endless stretches of wild grass swept by torrential rains."

It was now September (1935) and already cold wind was whipping from the high Tibetan plateaus, adding to the suffering of the staggering army as it waded through the almost constant rain. The largest part of the Grasslands was quicksand that could swallow anyone unlucky enough to venture into it. The only way across was by a few secret trails that followed some hard ridges hidden under the grass.

The Red Army vanguard were unable to find the trails, but they succeeded in capturing some aborigines and forced them under pain of death into guiding them across the marshes. At first the natives ignored the death threats, but later they became convinced that the quickest way to rid themselves of this enemy was to show them the way out.

Even with this aid, it was a hellish trip. Men slipped and

sank out of sight in the filthy black mud and water. Others developed hideous sores from impurities in the mud. Many fell exhausted and died in their tracks. Others caught pneumonia and choked to death as they struggled to keep up.

In later years when Mao was asked his own impressions of the death march through the Grasslands, he replied, "All I can remember is that I had difficulty crossing it once, while Chu Teh crossed it three times."

The army struggled through the Grasslands for ten days, losing a thousand men a day. The losses were greater during this awful period than at any other corresponding time during the Long March.

Even after passing the dreaded Grasslands, they were not permitted to rest. They fought a major battle with a Kuomintang army that tried to cut them off, and then still another and even bloodier battle with provisional troops before crossing the Chingling Mountains into Shensi Province at last.

The southern part of the province was under Kuomintang domination. The Red Army skirted the Kuomintang territory and moved along the western border of the state to circle back to Paoan, in the north part of the province. There they combined with a small Communist soviet where their welcome was genuine.

The first phase of the Long March was over. Mao arrived in Shensi with about 20,000 men. However, many of them were recruits picked up along the way. While no exact figures are available, an estimate claims that no more than seven thousand of the original hundred thousand who left Kiangsi finally arrived in Paoan. All those lost were not dead, however. There were more desertions than Mao ever admitted. In addition, the badly wounded were always left with peasant partisans who cared for them. Many recovered and joined Communist partisan groups themselves.

Mao's direct route from Kiangsi to Paoan was six thousand miles. He climbed eighteen mountain ranges, five of which were glacial. He made twenty-four major river crossings, and some factions of his army fought a battle every day of the year they marched.

The most important thing he accomplished, of course, was the preservation intact of the Red Army. This gave him a base upon which to rebuild for the future successful conquest of China. The second most important thing that came out of the Long March was that it exposed a vast number of Chinese in the western provinces to Mao and his policies. It made him millions of friends in those areas among people who had formerly looked upon the warring Communists as just another warlord army like those they had suffered under for so many years. This friendship was due directly to Mao's policy of forcing his troops to treat the peasants courteously and to pay for everything taken from them. Later, when the Red Army began its final push to destroy the Kuomintang, the friendship built during the Long March aided in the final victory.

In Paoan, Mao settle down to extensive and intensive political work, aimed mainly at solidifying his own grasp on the Communist Party.

In the meantime, Ho Lung was driven out of his north Hunan soviet. Beginning a long march of his own, the former bandit chief joined Chang Kuo-tao and Chu Teh in western Szechuan. Now their combined armies met the full fury of Chiang Kai-shek's forces. It soon became clear that they could not hold out. Despite Chang's reluctance, Chu Teh and Ho Lung finally persuaded him that their only hope was to join Mao in Shensi Province. They trekked across the Grasslands and over the Chingling Mountains where the armies recombined in October 1936.

Chu Teh resumed his former position as commander-in-chief of the Red Army. Chang Kuo-tao was never able to reconcile himself to Mao's domination. He eventually deserted to the Kuomintang and later went into exile in Hong Kong. Li Teh returned to Germany and today lives in East Berlin. Po Ku faded from the ranks of Mao's competitors.

Fighting continued in Shensi, but on a relatively minor

scale. Mao was able to clear the Kuomintang out of the walled city of Yenan, which became the Communist capital. The city was destroyed to a large extent and Mao lived in a cave dug into the loess hills. A number of American writers came to visit him there. Very conscious of the need for good world opinion, he affably received them all.

The south part of Shensi was controlled by Chang Hsueh-liang, the Young Marshal. He was the son of Chang Tso-lin, the Old Marshal, who had been warlord of Manchuria until killed by the Japanese. The Young Marshal had been run out of Manchuria by the Japanese in 1932. From Shensi, he maintained tenuous ties with the Kuomintang. He was exceptionally bitter toward Japan.

Mao also considered the Japanese a greater enemy than even Chiang Kai-shek. Japan turned Chinese Manchuria into the Japanese puppet state of Manchukuo in 1932 and planned an all-out attack on China proper. So, instead of planning new attacks on Chiang's Nationalist Chinese government, Mao Tse-tung sought a new plan whereby the Red Army could cooperate with Chiang's Kuomintang Army against the Japanese.

The situation suddenly took a dramatic turn in December, 1936. Unable to transport a large enough army into Shensi to defeat the Communists, Chiang Kai-shek tried to pressure the Young Marshal into attacking Mao in Yenan. Chang Hsueh-liang, on the other hand, was obsessed with the idea of driving the Japanese out of his father's old dominion of Manchuria. He did not want to waste his strength in fighting other Chinese.

When his letters and emissaries failed to move Chang, Chiang suddenly flew to Sian to see the Young Marshal. Chang became enraged when Chiang angrily rejected a demand that the Kuomintang Army attack the Japanese. He had Chiang arrested along with members of the generalissimo's party.

The first Mao heard of Chiang Kai-shek's detention was

when Chang Ksueh-liang announced that he intended to have Chiang tried by a people's court for his failure to protect the Chinese from Japanese aggression. He invited the Communists to participate in the trial of their old enemy.

It would appear that Mao would have welcomed the opportunity to rid himself of the man who had been trying to exterminate the Chinese Communist Party for the last nine years. However, Mao and Chou En-lai were horrified. Both Communist leaders were convinced that Japan was on the verge of launching an all-out war to conquer China. Japanese maneuvers in Manchuria pointed toward this. Both also knew that Japan would win unless the Chinese were able to put up a total defense. It would be necessary for the Kuomintang Nationalists and the Chinese Communists temporarily to set aside their own struggle and unite against this common foreign danger.

In a hastily-called meeting of the Central Committee in Yenan, Mao argued that Chiang Kai-shek was essential to the defense of China. Just as he had always worked toward making use of his enemies in the Communist Party, Mao now proposed to make use of Chiang Kai-shek. He pointed out to his fellow leaders that if Chiang should be executed by the Young Marshal, the Kuomintang Party would probably collapse. Chiang had succeeded in bringing all the various warlords under his control. They would not stand for anyone else's taking command but would start fighting among themselves for the supreme position. The result would be political and military chaos that would permit the Japanese to achieve an easy victory, for the Red Army would not be strong enough to stop them.

Mao was his party's Secretary, the premier position at that time, but he was not a dictator. He was described as the "first among equals." He could not order the Central Committee to follow his directives; he could only persuade. In this case they agreed that Chiang's most likely successor, Ho Ying-chin, would not be able to hold the Kuomintang together. And even if he did, there was little chance of the Communists' ever being able to make a united front with him against the Japanese. They agreed with Mao that it was imperative that Chiang's life be spared and that he be returned to Peking.

Negotiations for Chiang's life were entrusted to Chou En-lai. Chou rushed to Sian, as did Madame Chiang Kai-shek. Chou bluntly told the Young Marshal that he could expect no Communist support for trying Chiang, and that Mao Tse-tung was determined to bring about a coalition between the Kuomintang and the Red Army to fight the Japanese. Chang Hsueh-liang gave in to Chou En-lai.

From that point on, Chou conducted all negotiations with Chiang Kai-shek. Chiang was told that he had to form a common front with Mao against the Japanese. The generalissimo angrily refused. But as time went on he became convinced that he had to deal with the Communists.

Chiang was released. It was claimed at the time that he made no deals. This may have been done to save Chiang's face, for within two months of his return to Peking he was negotiating with Mao for the united front that the Communists were demanding. Under the agreement finally reached by Chiang Kai-shek and Chou En-lai, the Nationalist government would release all political prisoners, grant additional civil liberties, stop fighting the Communists, and join the Red Army in trying to repulse the invading Japanese.

Mao, in turn, agreed to end his rebellion and to permit the Nationalist government to control Communist-held areas. In addition, Mao agreed to stop seizing land from rich landowners and to permit the Red Army to become part of the Nationalist forces.

Chu Teh, Lin Piao and Peng Teh-Huai went with the Red Army, which became the Chinese Eighth Route Army. Chiang, however, had been forced into this collaboration and distrusted Mao. So he was careful to keep the Red's Eighth Route Army subordinated. Despite the suspicion, the united effort was reasonably successful for two years, but after 1939 Chiang began treating the Communists like enemies again.

During those years Mao Tse-tung remained in Yenan and

Mao is shown in Yenan in 1938 writing his famous book "On Protracted War." *China Pictorial Photo.*

took no part in military operations. His work was entirely political and literary. In 1938 he completed his famous book *On Protracted War,* in which he dealt with the principles of guerrilla warfare and the Communist philosophy of war in general.

The following sections, taken from *Quotations from Chairman Mao Tse-tung,* published by the Foreign Languages Press, Peking, 1972 edition (the translation of the famous "little red book"), show the basis of Mao's military philosophy:

History shows that wars are divided into two kinds, just and unjust. All wars that are progressive are just, and all wars that impede progress are unjust. [He means here that if war advances Communist principles, it is just, and if it does not, than it is unjust.] We Communists oppose all unjust wars that impede progress, but we do not oppose progressive just wars. Not only do we Communists not oppose just wars, we actively participate in them.

. . . It can therefore be said that politics is war without bloodshed, while war is politics with bloodshed.

Revolutionary war is an antitoxin which not only eliminates the enemy's poison but also purges us of our own filth. Every just, revolutionary war is endowed with tremendous power and can transform many things or clear the way for their transformation.

Later in 1938, writing in *Problems of War and Stategy,* Mao summed up his philosophy in the words "Every Communist must grasp the truth, 'Political power grows out of the barrel of a gun.' "

Another prominent Communist was also making a name for himself as a writer on theoretical Communism. He was Liu Shao-chi. At Yenan Liu became second only to Mao in the Party's hierarchy. Eventually he would shove Mao aside and for five years would head the Party before Mao would be able to regain his former position.

Liu was a slender man with a perpetually mournful expression. For some peculiar reason, he disliked to bare his head. He wore an army cap indoors and out. Like Mao, Liu came from peasant stock in Hunan. He was introduced to Communism while a student in Peking University and joined the Party when it was formed in 1921. He then went to Moscow for study. After his return Liu worked with Li Li-san in organizing coal miners in the Kiangsi-Hunan region. He was in Kiangsi when the Long March began but apparently went to Shanghai when Mao began his long trek to Shensi Province.

In later years, when it was fashionable to have made the March, Party propaganda claimed that Liu was a March veteran, but this does not appear to be true. He rejoined Mao after the Red Army reached Yenan. Liu was a very able man, a good organizer and administrator as well as a brilliant theoretician. As a writer, he was considered Mao's equal. However, he represented the party faction that still embraced the Li Li-san line of proletarianism. Mao, who represented the peasant-farmer faction, apparently felt that it was wise to include his opponents in high party positions for the sake of unity. In any event, Liu became the number two man in the Chinese Communist Party and was regarded as Mao's successor.

About that time there appeared in Yenan another person who would have a profound effect upon Mao's life. This was a woman, an actress, who had already had three husbands when she saw Mao Tse-tung and decided that he would be her fourth husband.

This woman, who would one day prove to be a most remarkable person, was called Lan Pin (meaning "Blue Apple") as an actress, but became Chiang Ching after coming to Yenan in 1938. She was born in Shangtung of poor parents about 1912, give or take a few years one way or the other. She never was very much interested in pinpointing her age. She first became known when she became a librarian and married a young Communist who introduced her to Marxism. In 1934, Chiang Ching and her husband were arrested by Chiang Kai-shek's police. After their release, her husband deserted her. She went to Shanghai, where she became a movie actress, appearing as Nora in a Chinese version of Ibsen's famous play *A Doll's House*, which dealt with women's emancipation. She then married a movie critic named Tang Na.

When the Japanese attacked Shanghai in 1937, Chiang Ching left her husband and eventually arrived in Yenan. There a minor Party official named Kang Sheng, who had known her family in Shangtung, got her a job as instructor at the local art academy. It was there, while Mao was lecturing to the students, that Chiang Ching first met him. Mao could not help noticing the pretty woman who clapped louder, took more notes and seemed more impressed than all the others. Later he spoke to her about her interest. She said that she wanted more instruction in Marxism. Mao invited her to come to the cave he used as a home whenever she had time and he would personally instruct her.

Chiang Ching came—and after a while she stayed. This shocked the rather puritanical members of the Central Committee, for Chinese Communism had always been a sort of sexless society. Later, Mao decided that he wanted to divorce his wife Ho. She had never fully recovered from the rigors of the Long March and had gone to Moscow for treatment. Ho was highly regarded by other members of the Central Committee, and there was naturally strong opposition to Mao's discarding her to marry an actress.

This is not a book that intends to pry into the skeletons in the personal closets of the people it deals with. The important things in a man's life are those that influence and change the lives of a people or alter the course of history. In the case of Mao Tse-tung, his infatuation with Chiang Ching did indeed have a profound effect upon the course of Chinese Communism. It is quite possible Mao Tse-tung would never have been able to fight his way back to the top after he was deposed in the 1960s if it had not been for the iron will and crafty maneuvering of his "Blue Apple." Because of this, Chiang Ching is important in any story of the life of Mao Tse-tung and any account of Chinese Communism. She was and is a remarkable woman.

John Roderick of the Associated Press visited Yenan a short time after this. He reported: "Mao was reported to have gone from cave to cave in Yenan begging for the support of Chu Teh, Hsu Teh-li, and Chou's wife, Ten Ying-chao, in his plan to divorce the ill and absent Ho and marry Chiang Ching. He threatened, if he failed, to return to his native village and become a farmer."

Although the Party's number two man, Liu Shao-chi,

vigorously opposed the divorce and remarriage, Mao won his point. However, the Central Committee insisted that Chiang Ching be barred from any Party activities.

Just why this prohibition was placed on Mao and his new wife is not known. In any event, Chiang Ching scrupulously observed the restriction for twenty years and broke it only to fight like a tigress to restore Mao after he was downgraded by Liu Shao-chi and Liu's followers.

In time Mao and Chiang Ching would have two daughters. Previously he had had two children by Yang Kai-hui, his "proud poplar," and five by Ho Tzu-chen. Of his nine children, a son by Yang Kai-hui and two daughters by Chiang Ching are the only known survivors. Three of his children by Ho Tzu-chen were left with peasants at the beginning of the Long March. All efforts to trace them later proved fruitless.

The Chinese were driven steadily back as the Japanese Army captured Peking and then drove south and west. Fighting was severe in the beginning, but after Pearl Harbor Chiang, confident that the United States would eventually defeat Japan, was more interested in preserving his army and amassing material for resumption of the civil war with the Communists after World War II ended. Despite pressure from President Franklin D. Roosevelt of the United States and needling from General Joseph Stillwell of the United States Army, Chiang continued his policy of "trading space for time" by retreating before the advance of the Japanese.

Meanwhile, the United States poured millions of dollars worth of supplies into China via the famous Burma Road and by aircraft flying "the hump" over the Himalaya Mountains from India. In the meantime, the graft, corruption and exploitation of the people by Kuomintang officials and army officers became so bad that all respect for the government was destroyed. This naturally played directly into the hands of Mao Tse-tung.

The Japanese resistance collapsed suddenly in August,

1945, after the United States destroyed Hiroshima and Nagasaki, Japan, with atom bombs. Until a short time before the first bomb was exploded in a test in New Mexico no one really knew for sure if it would work. Therefore military planning had been based upon the necessity for making an invasion of the Japanese home islands. China was to be a major base from which this amphibious landing would be made. Expectations called for as much as a million-man casualty rate during the invasion. Chiang expected this to result in the United States' pushing the Japanese out of China and Manchuria before the invasion of the homeland. Then Chiang's plan called for his army, which he had struggled to keep intact all through World War II, to turn suddenly and wipe out the Red Army.

The unexpected end of the war, in August, 1945, changed all this. Mao had been making his own careful plans during these years, just as Chiang Kai-shek had. The Red Army had gained strength during the war instead of losing it. The Communist Eighth Route Army increased from 45,000 in 1937 to nearly a half million by 1945. The New Fourth Front Red Army had been attacked and nearly destroyed by Chiang Kai-shek's troops while trying to ford the Yangtze in 1941, but by 1945 it had been reinforced and expanded by Chen Yi as general and Liu Shao-chi as political commissar until it numbered over 150,000.

The Red Army managed to capture a large store of weapons and ammunition from the surrendering Japanese Army despite all Chiang Kai-shek could do to stop it. Later, Russia pulled out of Manchuria, leaving an enormous stockpile of captured Japanese munitions, which Lin Piao took over. This was the only real help Mao had ever received from Russia.

It was obvious that both Chiang and Mao were maneuvering for resumption of the Chinese civil war. President Truman worked hard to prevent it, sending first Ambassador Patrick J. Hurley and then General George C. Marshall to China. Marshall was able to persuade Mao to fly to

General George C. Marshall reviewing troops in Yenan in 1946 with a group of Chinese Communist officials. Marshall was on a peace mission as a special representative of President Harry S. Truman. From left are: Gen. Chou En-Lai, Marshall, Gen. Chu Teh, Gen. Lin Piao, and Mao Tse-tung. *Wide World Photos.*

Chungking for a meeting with Chiang. It came to nothing because Chiang was determined to destroy Communism in China.

The flight was Mao's first trip in an airplane. He was awed by the beauty of the Chinese landscape as seen from the sky. In a burst of emotion, he wrote one of his most famous poems. It is called "The Snow." Poetry loses in translation unless the translator is as great a poet as the original author. Even then, the differences in languages makes it almost impossible for a translator to capture the exact shades of meaning in the original. Consequently translations of "The Snow" do not strike the reader with the impact said to be contained in the Chinese version.

In the poem Mao speaks of the thousand acres beyond the Great Wall, all locked in ice and snow. He then compares the reddish earth to a flush-faced girl dressed in white garments, and how the beauty of the landscape calls many heroes to pursue her. He ends by recalling famous emperors from Shih Huang to Genghis Khan and how they lacked a true feeling for their country. He concluded by saying that not until now have men had a true love for the earth. The unspoken inference is that this true love came from the communistic spirit.

John Roderick, who visited Yenan during that time, described Mao as he looked in 1947: "He retained the look of youth in his round face. His hair, receding in front, gave him the high forehead which was one of the distinguishing features of his later years. His eyes, hidden behind narrowed lids, peered at the world quizzically, without hostility, but with no particular warmth. The mole, which became more prominent later, was visible on his chin . . . . He looked confident, resourceful, thoughtful and not especially ferocious."

When the Marshall Mission failed, Chiang launched a three-pronged attack against the Communists. One was in Manchuria against Lin Piao's corps. The second was in Shantung against Chen Yi's army. The third was against Yenan. Lin and Chen stopped the Nationalists' thrusts without trouble, but Yenan was inadequately defended. Mao and the Central Committee fled north to a little town near the Great Wall of China until Yenan could be retaken, in late 1948.

· From this point on, the civil war turned sharply against Chiang. The Communist advance was steady. It was not the Nationalists who were on the defensive. Mao in Yenan told Roderick, "Come and visit me in Peking in two years."

12
Triumph!

On January 31, 1949, the Manchurian legions of Lin Piao marched unopposed into Peking, which was called Peiping by the Nationalists. They then moved south, driving the Nationalist troops south of the Yangtze. There they paused to regroup and wait for orders. In Yenan Mao waited until he was sure that Lin's troops were in Peking to stay. Then he and the Central Committee moved to the Chinese capital on March 25, 1949. He entered riding in an open jeep. He wore a long coat with a fur collar and a cap with the earflaps turned up. He rode standing up, occasionally raising his hand to wave at cheering soldiers lining his way.

Chu Teh rode in another jeep directly behind Mao. The Red Army commander-in-chief smiled broadly throughout the procession. Behind Chu Teh came Liu Shao-chi and Chou En-lai. Mao drove on to his new home, a small palace within the Forbidden City behind Tien An Men gate. The palace had originally been built for a Turkish princess acquired by a

Chinese emperor for his harem, but the unfortunate girl aroused the enmity of the emperor's mother, who strangled her. The place was known as the Palace of the Fragrant Concubine. It has been Mao's personal home ever since.

Mao waited nearly a month, until April 21, to give Lin Piao orders to cross the Yangtze. The Red Army, a million strong, forded the river against slight opposition and two days later had captured Nanking and Taiyuan. Then in May they took Hangchow, Nanchang and Shanghai. Tsingtao fell in June, with Foochow and Lanchow following in August. Everywhere, Kuomintang resistance was crumbling.

Chiang issued a statement that he was cleaning out corruption in his Nationalist government. However, it was an empty claim since he depended for support on the very men he would have been forced to purge. After Lin Piao took Canton, Chiang resigned as president of Nationalist China but kept control of the army and the treasury. He then "retired" to Taiwan, where he set up a rival Chinese government after the total defeat of his forces on the mainland.

On October 1, 1949, with all the mainland except a small area under his control, Mao Tse-tung, together with Chu Teh, Liu Chao-chi, Chou En-lai and other members of the Central Committee, climbed to the pavilion atop Tien An Men, the "Gate of Heavenly Peace." The great square before the gate was jammed with cheering people as far as Mao could see. Police had forced the crowd back from the wide street in front. A seemingly endless flow of soldiers marched past.

The day before, the Central Committee had held a final meeting to hammer out the details of reorganization. Mao again emerged the number one man but still not a total dictator. He was subordinate to the will of the majority of the Committee. His new title was Chairman of the People's Republic of China. Liu was made vice-chairman. Chou En-lai became premier and foreign minister. Chu Teh remained commander-in-chief of the Red Army.

There was considerable division among the Central Com-

Mao reads proclamation establishing the People's Republic of China on October 1, 1949.

mittee members, but in this moment of supreme triumph they all rallied behind Mao Tse-tung. They stood in a silent line back of him when Mao stepped to a bank of microphones atop Tien An Men and in a low voice read a proclamation proclaiming the People's Republic of China.

Mao was then just three months short of his fifty-sixth birthday. Forty years had passed since he left his village at the age of 16. Twenty-eight years had passed since he huddled with his fellow conspirators on a picnic boat to form the Chinese Communist Party. And it had been but fourteen years since he struggled into Shensi at the end of the Long March. He had grown heavier. His hair had receded. His face had lost the dreamy look his earlier photographs show. But he still looked more like a prosperous farmer than the ruler of the largest—in population—nation on earth.

Mao now faced the gigantic task of making himself and his government secure. He knew that he had won a victory but still had to insure that the victory would be permanent. In a speech delivered in 1949, Mao said, "The imperialists and domestic reactionaries will certainly not take their defeat lying down and will struggle to the last ditch. After there is peace and order throughout the country, they will still engage in sabotage and create disturbances in various ways and will try every day and every minute to stage a comeback. This is inevitable and beyond all doubt, and under no circumstances must we relax our vigilance."

Then, in another speech to the Central Committee in 1949, Mao said, "After the enemies with guns have been wiped out, there will still be enemies without guns; they are bound to struggle desperately against us, and we must never regard these enemies lightly. If we do not now raise and understand the problem in this way, we shall commit the gravest mistakes."

Although Mao had always maintained a policy of trying to conquer his enemies by persuasion, he could be bloodily ruthless when the occasion demanded, as when he put down the mutiny in Kiangsi. Now he instituted a reign of terror to wipe out all opposition as quickly as possible. This was necessary in order to prevent Chiang Kai-shek from using the resistance groups to make a comeback on the mainland.

Also, Mao feared foreign attempts to take advantage of China's weakness. He did not want to have his army tied down in constant internal warfare.

According to Robert Payne, "The extent of the terror which swept over China during the first year of Communist power will probably never be known. It reached down into the most remote villages, and in one way or another affected the lives of nearly everyone on the mainland . . . . Quite deliberately Mao chose the weapon of terror to ensure the permanence of the Communist revolution . . . ."

In his famous speech "On the Correct Handling of Contradictions Among the People," delivered in 1957, Mao claimed that 800,000 Kuomintang supporters had been "liquidated" in the mass purge that extended from 1949 until 1954. Payne quotes Po Yi-po, vice chairman of the Economic Affairs Committee, as putting the figure at two million.

Mao did not personally direct the bloody purges. He set them in motion and then, two months after proclaiming the Republic, he departed for Moscow to come to terms with Stalin.

Stalin and Mao had never liked each other. Stalin had always backed Chiang Kai-shek and had contemptuously told General George C. Marshall, "The Chinese Communist Party is a radish: red on the outside, but white inside." Now, however, Stalin was forced to cooperate, since the Chinese Communist Party victory was assured. Mao, in turn, badly needed foreign support. He had to do something about starvation, devastation from floods, and China's backward technology. Technological help could come only from Russia.

Mao spent two months in Russia, and that was his first trip outside China. He had several meetings with Stalin but spent most of his time visiting Russian factories, observing their operation. In the end, Stalin grudgingly gave China a credit of $300,000,000 and provided several thousand Russian technicians to teach the Chinese how to develop their industries. Mao, remembering the troubles he had had with Russian advisers from the old Comintern, was not happy over that large influx of Russians into China, but he had no choice; he had to put China's economy on a firm basis. Otherwise he could expect internal disorder that would encourage foreign powers to move in.

Mao returned to China to face a new crisis. Already the Red Army had assembled a fleet of junks to drive Chiang Kai-shek out of Taiwan. The island had been Chinese territory until it was seized by the Japanese. The announced American policy was that the United States would not fight to support Chiang. However, in June, 1950, before Mao could launch his cross-channel attack on Taiwan, North Korea was egged by Russia into attacking South Korea.

Korea had been split at the 38th Parallel into a Communist North and a Democratic South at the end of World War II. Now Russia was attempting to reunite the country under a Communist government. President Harry Truman immediately committed American troops to the defense of South Korea and persuaded the United Nations to go to war in support of the Republic of Korea as well.

At the same time Truman ordered the United States Seventh Fleet to prevent any Communist China attacks on Taiwan. That forced Mao to call off his intended attack.

In the beginning, United Nations Forces in Korea, operating under the command of General Douglas MacArthur, were pushed back to a small area known as the Beachhead, in South Korea. It appeared at that time that North Korean Communist forces would push the defenders into the sea. Then MacArthur, in one of the most brilliant maneuvers in modern military history, made a landing at Inchon, near the South Korean capital of Seoul. The maneuver split the overextended North Korean army and sent them reeling back. By November, United Nations forces had taken most of

North Korea and were approaching the Yalu River, which was the border between North Korea and China's Manchuria.

Suddenly, in late November, American commanders began reporting clashes with Chinese troops, and by December a flood of Red Army troops were pouring across the Yalu. United Nations forces were hurled back across the 38th Parallel before they finally were able to regain the offensive. The combined Chinese and North Korean armies were driven back, and the fighting line stabilized just above the Parallel.

The reasons for Chinese intervention in the Korean War are still being argued. There was a report that Mao Tse-tung debated with himself for three days before giving permission for Chinese intervention. The basic plan and enthusiasm for the Chinese attack have been credited to Lin Piao.

There were actually several reasons for the Chinese gamble in Korea. One of course was that Communist China did not want to see an oriental Communist nation go down in defeat to the West. Mao felt this would have a bad effect upon the Chinese people. Also, Mao had always hated Russia. When Russia, after instigating the Korean War, failed to come adequately to North Korea's assistance, Mao felt it would make the Russians lose face and build China's prestige in the worldwide Communist movement if she came to North Korea's aid. Stalin had already considered the possibility of Mao's China challenging his Russia's leadership in the world Communist movement at some future time. Chinese intervention in Korea was a definite bid in that direction. It served notice on small Communist countries that China could be depended upon to aid her Marxist brothers, while Russia could not.

Also, it has been suggested that China was in a state of turmoil at that time. The reign of terror was at its height. The land reform program was under way. Mao needed a strong foreign threat to rally the Chinese people behind him as they had rallied behind Chiang Kai-shek when the Japanese attacked China in 1937. There was also the age-old problem of what to do with a million trained soldiers after a war ends.

Once Mao had set the Korean intervention in motion, he

had nothing more to do with it. The actual fighting was the responsibility of Lin Piao and Peng Teh-huai, who had replaced Chu Teh as Defense Minister. The foreign implications were handled by Chou En-lai. Mao devoted himself to domestic problems.

He began his Communist regime by reassuring property owners that private property would be respected, and—where it was necessary to nationalize—would be paid for. He felt it necessary to move slowly to avoid disrupting the national economy, which was in a disastrous state anyway. Land reform was vigorously carried out. Large absentee landowners were tried by local peasant courts, and a large number of them were executed. Strict new laws stopped speculation and stabilized prices. Heavy industry was nationalized, but in many cases the former managers remained as managers under the Communists. Next, private banks were nationalized and replaced by state banks.

There was a great need for labor as the industrial revolution got into full swing. Soldiers not being used in Korea or for hunting down "Kuomintang bandits" were impressed in work batallions. This was done against the will of Defense Minister Peng Teh-huai, who felt that the guerrilla training of the past was insufficient to meet the challenge of modern warfare. He wanted his soldiers used for training rather than work. His wishes were ignored by Mao.

European trading companies had been permitted to remain, as had foreign missionaries. But as the economy improved, Mao subtly drove both out. The merchants found themselves saddled with such high taxes and demands for wage increases that they had to quit or face bankruptcy. Likewise, Mao did not abolish religion, but his propagandists worked among the Chinese Christians, convincing them that Chinese and not foreigners should run their churches.

Many of Mao's actions during that period were intended only as gradual steps toward complete Marxism. As soon as he felt safe, he stopped the terror and wholesale executions.

People convicted of anticommunism were sentenced to labor battalions instead of the firing squads, and were given a chance to "rectify" themselves through a study of Marxism.

Then the shocked peasants, who had been so proud of the little farms they had gotten under the land reform, saw their land taken from them and lumped into cooperatives. The peasants themselves became no more than farm workers on government acres. The resulting disturbances were so bad that Mao was forced to bend a little. Love of the land is deeply engrained in the Chinese peasant. Mao broke the large labor battalions into smaller groups, who were given more control over what they planted and how they cultivated the farms. Also, each peasant was given his personal plot of ground. It was small, only large enough to grow some vegetables for his own table and to hold a pig sty and a chicken yard. However, it satisfied the age-old yearning for land.

Mao realized there would be opposition to collectivization of the peasants. In the beginning he tried to operate with private ownership of farms. Unfortunately, the tiny individual farms could not be operated efficiently. The government was faced with a Herculean task of trying to feed China's increasing millions. In 1954 a government census placed the population at close to six hundred million, with an annual increase of about twelve million. Food production had to be raised.

The next step was to turn the collective farms into communes. A commune became a self-supporting unit. In addition to the collective operation of giant farms, each commune built its own roads, hospitals, factories, and even homes for the aged.

The commune system, which added additional regimentation, was vigorously resisted also. Thousands of refugees fled to British Hong Kong during that period. The peasant dissatisfaction was coupled with disastrous floods and famines and droughts in the late 1950s, which further eroded Mao's position. The fall in food production coincided with the

Mao rarely lets himself be photographed without his drab coat buttoned to the top. This rare shot made in 1958 when he visited a commune shows him in pleated slacks and an open collar shirt, leaning on a hoe handle as he joined in farm work. *China Pictorial Photo*.

failure of Mao's "Great Leap Forward," which was intended to increase China's industrial capacity dramatically. Industrial development was further hampered by increasing quarrels with Russia, which ended in Russia's recalling all of her technicians from China.

Mao's troubles began in 1957 and came to a head in 1959. For years the West had considered Mao a Stalin-type absolute dictator. This was not true. Mao held his power and place at the top through the support of the majority of the Central Committee. While some of the members, Liu Shao-chi, for example, voted according to their own best interests, others like Chou En-lai and Chu Teh voted for what they considered best for China. The result was that the latter two voted either with or against Mao Tse-tung, according to their own convictions. Both had supported Mao at Tsunyi in Mao's last major showdown with the Party but failed to do so when Liu Shao-chi challenged Mao's leadership in 1959.

Mao's difficulties came from two of his best-intentioned activities. One was the Great Leap Forward, which failed. The other was his attempt to lighten some of the political repression and permit criticism of his regime.

In February Mao made a speech called "On the Correct Handling of Contradictions." In that speech he invited the Chinese people to tell him what was wrong with their government. It was a startling action for a dictator.

"The only way to settle questions of an ideological nature or controversial issues among the people is by the democratic method, the method of discussion, of criticism, of persuasion and education, and not by the method of coercion or repression."

He told his audience that the government must "let a hundred flowers blossom and a hundred schools of thought contend."

"The policy of letting a hundred flowers blossom and a hundred schools of thought contend is designed to promote the flourishing of the arts and the progress of science . . . .

Different forms and styles in art can develop freely, and different schools in science can contend freely. We think that it is harmful to the growth of art and science if administrative measures are used to impose one particular style of art or school of thought and to ban the other."

Mao's speech was not immediately printed in its entirety but was "explained" in the press. People showed a natural reluctance to come forward and start criticizing. The executions of the 800,000 dissenters after Mao took over were still fresh in everybody's memory. The government actually had to mount a propaganda campaign to start the "hundred flowers" blossoming.

However, once the initial fear was allayed that the statement was a trap to ferret out dissenters, the flood of criticisms inundated the government. Mao was said to have been stunned both by the amount and the ferocity of the criticism. He had been aware that there was some resentment among the intellectuals, but he had not dreamed that it was as widespread and deep as it then appeared to be.

Students bitterly resented having to spend more time studying political propaganda than in academic studies. Professors ranted about government and party restrictions on what they could teach. A vast number of complaints centered on arrogant and dictatorial attitudes of Party leaders on lower levels.

Here are a few examples of specific complaints, quoted by Roderick MacFarquhar in *The Hundred Flowers Campaign and the Chinese Intellectuals:*

Principal, Hupeh Medical College: "Many problems that exist in the institutions of higher learning today are attributable to the inappropriateness of the Party committee system. The Party committee monopolizes everything, insisting on having a finger in every pie, and yet knows very little about the business of teaching . . ."

Advisor, Supreme People's Court: "Also the punishments meted out are subject to the whims and fancies of the court . . ."

Professor, Institute of Chinese Medicine: "Doctors seldom have time to engage in research work, their main duty being to attend [political indoctrination meetings]."

Criticisms continued to mount. In early June, student unrest broke out in a number of schools and universities. In one case students crowded the streets with signs reading, "Welcome Back to Chiang Kai-shek!" Elsewhere, teachers were overpowered and humiliated.

As the unrest spread, Mao suddenly clamped down on criticism, rescinded the principles of his "hundred flowers campaign," and deployed police and army to restore order. Strict censorship and political thought control were reestablished.

The rise and fall of leadership in the Chinese Communist Party since its founding in 1921 shows that a leader in the Party can hold his position only as long as he is right. Once he begins to make errors, the coalition of different factions in the Central Committee gangs up on him. He is voted out. Sometimes he is disgraced and forced to go back to political "school" as Li Li-san was sent to Moscow for reindoctrination.

Ever since Tsunyi, Mao Tse-tung had been right. The Mao line had turned the Communist Party from ragged refugees to rulers of China. But now Mao was making mistakes. Both the "hundred flowers campaign" and the failure of the "Great Leap Forward" put Mao in the loser column.

It was now only a matter of time before his enemies in the Central Committee would put him and his policies on trial. The leader of the anti-Mao faction was Liu Chao-chi, the vice-chairman. Liu had always been a Li Li-sanist who favored the proletariat, while Mao favored the peasants. However, he had subordinated his own line to support Mao in the long years between the arrival in Shensi and the "hundred flowers campaign." The disruption following Mao's attempt to permit some relaxing of political repression gave Liu the opportunity he had sought so long.

Unfortunately for his enemies, Mao was too great a figure in

Communist China's history to be shunted aside as Chen Tu-hsiu, Li Li-san, and Po Ku had been. They had been little more than names to the rank and file of the Party. Mao was the George Washington of China. He had led a successful revolution and was revered by a great number of the Chinese masses. In a showdown Mao would retain public support. The army would probably follow the orders of Peng Teh-hui, the minister of defense, who had grown disenchanted with Mao along with Liu. However, the anti-Mao conspirators would be risking widespread disorders in support of Mao if they should depose him.

As a result, they moved slowly. Although Liu had made his decision in June at the conclusion of the "hundred flowers campaign," he did not challenge Mao in the Central Committee until April, 1959.

13
Mao's Personal Revolution

The rulers of the Chinese Communist Party have always made a policy of fighting their own personal battles in private. Very little has ever been revealed of the often titanic struggles that went on in the secret Central Committee meetings. This is specially true of the battle that ousted Mao Tse-tung from the top position in the Communist Party.

The brief glimpses inside the Committee chamber given by some of those present make it appear that the April, 1959, meeting opened with an address by Mao. He spoke on internal conditions in China and the progress made in establishing the farm communes. He was followed by vice-chairman Liu Shao-chi, who surprised Mao by making a bitter attack on Mao's leadership of the country. Mao fought back, defending his policies, including the ill-fated hundred flowers campaign.

The Central Committee had agreed to initiating the hundred flowers and therefore should have shared the blame for its failure with Mao Tse-tung. However, Mao did not remind them of this. He merely defended the basic idea of intellectual freedom. Actually, it is dangerous for any dictatorship to permit free expression. Mao had been motivated by two things. One was Premier Nikita Khrushchev's violent denunciation of the late Joseph Stalin in Russia. The new Russian ruler castigated Stalin and the grip of terror he held on his subordinates. Mao did not want the Chinese cursing his memory as the Russians now cursed Stalin's. Even more important, Mao was disturbed by the recent Hungarian revolt. Hungary had been a docile Russian satellite since the end of World War II. Suddenly the people, supposedly subservient, rose in a sudden burst of collective fury that brought about the complete collapse of the Hungarian Communist Party in a matter of two days. Communism in Hungary was saved only because Khrushchev rushed in army tanks to crush the revolt.

Mao was deeply affected by the fact the Hungarian Communist Party was so quickly undermined by bitter public dissatisfaction. Mao knew the Chinese peasants and their psychology very well indeed. He also knew students and their capacity for making trouble—even as he had made trouble for the government in his undergraduate days. He well knew that the peasants who resented losing their private land and the always rebellious students possessed the strength, if they could be properly organized, to turn China into another Hungary.

As far as removing peasant resentment was concerned, there was little he could do. He could not restore private ownership of the land, because the collective farms were more efficient and China had to increase food production. However, the Chinese peasants would present no threat unless they had leadership. The entire history of revolution, as Karl Marx knew, shows that every revolt of consequence has been led by a country's intellectuals, who play on the dissatisfaction of the mobs and masses. The "hundred flowers campaign," then, was an attempt to appease the dissatisfaction of the single group who could cause the most trouble. He realized that intellectual groups had to be given more freedom of expression.

Mao pointed out this fact in his original speech on handling contradictions, which launched the "Hundred Flowers":

> The experience of the Soviet Union shows that Stalin made the mistake of substituting internal difference for external antagonism, which resulted in a rule of terror and liquidation of thousands of Communists.
>
> In dealing with enemies, it is necessary to use force. We in China also have used force to deal with enemies of the people. The total of those liquidated by our security forces numbers 800,000. This is the figure up to 1954. [Mao spoke in April 1957]
>
> Since then we have no longer used methods of terror. Instead we have substituted persuasion and education. If one persists in using terror to solve internal antagonisms, it may lead to transformation of these antagonisms into antagonisms of the nation-enemy type, as happened in Hungary.

Mao's reasoning was commendable, but he was misinformed on the extent of dissatisfaction among China's disgruntled intellectuals. The storm of abusive criticism was so great that he had no choice but to cut it off and suppress the resulting student uprisings. Surprisingly, the dispossessed peasants, the group most likely to have resented Communism, were the greatest critics of the student revolts.

Now Mao Tse-tung paid the price for his good intentions. In the showdown vote he lost his leadership. However, his enemies could not risk mass reaction by dumping him entirely. He was permitted to keep his title of Chairman, but Liu Shao-chi took over direction of the Party and the nation. Mao Tse-tung became a powerless figurehead.

The power shift was done so smoothly and quietly that none outside the ruling hierachy of the Party knew that Mao had been demoted.

According to John Roderick, "Mao later complained that for the next six years, though he continued as Party chairman, neither Liu nor Teng Hsiao-ping consulted him on major policy matters." Teng Hsiao-ping was the Party's General Secretary.

During those six years as a figurehead, Mao continued to write, make speeches, and to appear before the world as the "ruler of Red China." They were eventful years. China's relations with Russia worsened. Mao's plan to build up heavy industry continued on a smaller scale, and China had trouble with India over the frontier between the two countries.

Earlier, Russia had promised to help China develop a nuclear capability. However, Khrushchev withdrew the promise in 1960. China then succeeded on her own in building an atomic bomb and successfully test-exploded it in 1964. It was said that the success was due in large measure to a Chinese scientist who had worked on the American program and then returned to China.

The development of a nuclear war capability moved China into the front ranks of the world's most powerful nations. Russia, worried over China's increasing military strength, tried to patch up her difficulties with China. Liu, who had been trained in Moscow, was agreeable, but Mao Tse-tung proved that he still had some influence by successfully leading a fight that went against Liu.

This battle in the Central Committee served notice on Liu and his supporters that Mao Tse-tung was not eliminated as a political force and a threat to their regime. As a result Liu and Teng began a subtle campaign to undermine Mao's position of veneration with the masses.

The opening maneuver was the performance of a play in Peking entitled, *Hai Jui Dismissed from Office*. It portrayed the injustice done to an army hero when he was removed from service by a dictatorial commander interested more in his own position than the welfare of the masses.

The hero, Hai Jui, was a thinly disguised portrait of Peng

Teh-huai, whom Mao Tse-tung had dismissed as defense minister when Peng objected to the use of his soldiers as farm workers. Peng had been a corps leader in the Long March and one of the top heroes of the revolution. The villainous official of the play was obviously Mao himself.

Mao realized that the play was the opening salvo in a campaign to discredit him with the Chinese people. Lin Piao, the current Defense Minister, was as disturbed as Mao, for Lin had been appointed to replace Peng Teh-huai by Mao. Lin had managed to retain his position under Liu, but the tone of the campaign against Mao indicated to Lin that he might well be in line to be purged himself.

Also working against Lin Piao was the fact that he had been a Maoist since before Tsunyi. He was a small, sour-faced man acknowledged to be a tactical military genius. Graduated from Chiang Kai-shek's Whampoa Academy at 19, he had joined the Communist Party in 1927 when he was 20 years old, and immediately came to Chu Teh's attention. He was promoted to company commander and then to regimental commander by the time he was 22, and the next year Chu Teh gave the 23-year-old command of an entire corps. Lin made the Long March as a corps commander on an equal footing with Peng Teh-huai and Lo Ping-hui. During World War II he was wounded in Manchuria and went to Moscow for treatment. One story claims that he got out of a sick bed to help the Russians fight the battle of Leningrad. Later, he returned to Manchuria to command the Red Army that swept south to capture Peking. After Peng Teh-huai was dismissed and disgraced by Mao for Peng's objections to the use of his army as common laborers, Lin Piao had become Defense Minister.

Lin had always been a good Communist and outwardly a Mao devotee. Yet inwardly he had been growing more and more dissatisfied with his own progress in the Party. He felt, probably with excellent reason, that his ability and services made him better qualified for Party leadership than those who occupied positions above him. Now in the battle shaping up between Liu Shao-chi and Mao Tse-tung, Lin Piao saw an opportunity to slip in ahead of Liu, Teng, Chou En-lai and his other superiors in the Party. And while it was not apparent at the time, he also saw an opportunity to step ahead of Mao Tse-tung as well.

Lin began planning his next moves as carefully as he ever had planned a battle. He was determined to lead a counter-revolution against Liu and the Central Committee. By carefully shifting top commanders, he had obtained a strong grip on the Red Army, and he thought he could control it. But he knew that he was not popular with the masses of China. He needed Mao Tse-tung and Mao's tremendous prestige to insure public support for his planned attack on Liu and his henchmen in the Red Chinese government.

Lin Piao did not approach Mao directly. He did not want to alert his enemies to the fact that he was plotting with Mao against them. He gave the impression of being a professional soldier who was above the politics of the moment. Instead, he had his wife, Yeh Chun, get in touch with Mao through Mao's wife, Chiang Ching.

At this stage Mao had only Lin Piao, Chiang Ching and Mao's political secretary, Chen Po-ta, on his side. But those three almost singlehandedly organized students into what became known as the Red Guard or "the Little Generals." Taking their cue from the student unrest and disorders during the "hundred flowers campaign," Lin and Chiang Ching worked secretly to arouse the young people to the threat against Mao. Mao was pictured as one who was being persecuted by "rightists" in the government.

Dissatisfied as they were by the present scheme of things and eager to fight anyone, thousands of young people secretly rallied to the Red Guard. If Liu was aware of the organization, he seemed to think it was nothing more than a means of indoctrinating young people with the spirit of Communism, for no government action was taken to prevent their formation.

While the youth were being formed into future shock troops

for the counterrevolution, Lin Piao began a campaign to deify Mao Tse-tung. He had thousands of little red books of Mao's quotations distributed to the army. The books were hailed as the essence of truth, and the soldiers were urged to read them to find the definite answer to political questions.

Mao seems to have doubted the wisdom of distributing these little red books. In a letter to Chiang Ching, he wrote, "Some of his [Lin Piao's] views have left me deeply troubled. I have never believed that those few little books of mine could have such fantastic magic."

However, Mao had no choice but to follow Lin Piao's lead at that point. And all Lin Piao had to support himself was Mao Tse-tung's enormous popularity with the masses of China. While Lin was Defense Minister with the army under his control, the army commanders were divided in their sympathies. Lin played on this division to use one faction of the army to suppress the other. He convinced his corps commanders that if they took part in what became known as the "Cultural Revolution" it would destroy the Red Army and lead to a takeover by Russia or Chiang Kai-shek. The army then stood neutral in the developing struggle between the Liu-Shao-chi-dominated Central Committee and Mao Tse-tung.

After several months of preparation, during which the cadres of Red Guard leaders were trained, Lin Piao began his attack with an editorial in the *Liberation Army Daily*, a paper published for the army. It violently denounced "rightists" in the government who were departing from the "correct" Mao Tse-tung line.

The editorial triggered youth uprisings patterned after those that happened during the "hundred flowers campaign," but more effective because these were planned and competently led, while the previous youth riots had been local and mainly spontaneous. The local police were unable to cope with them, and the army stayed aloof. The marauding youth stormed through the streets of China's principle cities, carrying huge poster pictures of Mao and waving copies of the

Members of China's Red Guard, wearing armbands and carrying books containing the sayings of Mao, parade through Peking streets during cultural revolution of 1966. *Wide World Photos*.

new bible, the little red book of *Quotations from Chairman Mao Tse-tung.*

Roderick reported, "The youths paraded their teachers naked through the streets, humiliated old men and women suspected of being 'bourgeois,' confiscated heirlooms, overturned gravestones, put politicians in dunce hats (perhaps one of the more sensible acts), broke into temples and burned Buddhist images."

In the beginning Mao stayed aloof from the disturbances, which Liu seemed to think were local only. It was not until it became apparent that the Red Guard was winning control that Mao came forward to give the Cultural Revolution his public blessing. On August 18, 1966, the word was spread to all Red Guard members in Peking to assemble in front of Tien An Men gate. More than a half-million jammed the square in front of the Gate of Heavenly Peace. They saw Mao Tse-tung and Lin Piao with Chiang Ching, Mao's wife, standing behind them. A teenage girl wearing a Red Guard armband stepped forward and pinned a Red Guard insignia on Mao's uniform.

The crowd went wild with enthusiasm. The shouts and cheers were unlike anything seen in China since Mao, standing in that same position atop the great gate, had proclaimed the People's Republic of China in October, 1949.

Ken Ling, a member of the Red Guard who later deserted to Chiang Kai-shek's Taiwan, described in his book, *The Revenge of Heaven*, how the Red Guards grew to nearly twenty million within a few months. Their numbers included college youth, high school teenagers, and even a large number of subteens.

Ken Ling told how students in cities away from Peking, where the Red Guard started, were brought together on the athletic fields, where loudspeakers played recordings of speeches. Many of the recordings were made by Chiang Ching.

"Mao's wife presented the meaning and aims of the Cultural Revolution," Ken Ling wrote. "To uproot revisionism completely. Many people, she said, had been 'raising the red flag to strike down the red flag.' She described the Cultural Revolution as historically without precedent . . . After the hour-long broadcast, the work team members addressed us, saying that schools would be closed so that students could join the 'Great Socialist Cultural Revolution.' "

The "work team members" mentioned were Lin Piao's trained cadres sent out to organize the youth.

Ken Ling goes on to say that each group formed had its own flag and marched in formation. The leader carried a Mao quotation on a poster, reading, "The thousand components of Marxism can be summed up in one sentence, 'Rebellion is justified. Based on this understanding, one should struggle, resist and make socialist revolution.' "

" 'Rebellion is justified' was our supreme guiding principle," says Ken Ling. "Sometimes when people criticized our excesses, all we had to do was raise the Mao quotation plaque in front of them and say, 'Open your eyes and take a hard look at what Chairman Mao teaches us to do!' "

Liu Shao-chi and his closest supporters were first placed under house arrest. Later Liu was dragged through the streets by Red Guards and put through a series of public "trials" for his "rightest" crimes. His wife was also subjected to three mock trials and public indignities. In 1967 Liu was forced to recant publicly his opposition to Mao Tse-tung. His public apology ended with: "Long live the great teacher, great leader, great supreme commander, Chairman Mao. A long, long life to him." It was said that Lin Piao wrote these words for Liu to parrot.

The Red Guard finally got so far out of hand that Lin Piao was forced to send in army units to restore order. Then in April, 1969, three years after Lin Piao's Liberation Army Daily sounded the call for social revolution, Mao was sufficiently in control to call the party to the Ninth National Party Congress. The government had to consider the future course of the Party and to hear a report on the serious border clash between Russian and Chinese troops on the Siberian-Manchurian border.

There were 1,500 delegates. The Congress reelected Mao Tse-tung as Chairman, endorsed the dismissal of Liu Shao-chi, enlarged the Central Committee to 25 members, and endorsed the election of a five-member Standing Committee of the Central Committee. The Standing Committee, in effect, rose above the Central Committee and thus became in actuality the real rulers of Red China. The five members elected were those who had led the Cultural Revolution: Mao Tse-tung, Lin Piao, Chou En-lai, Chen Po-ta, and Kang Sheng. Kang Sheng was a friend of Chiang Chang. Chiang Chang and Yeh Chun, Lin Piao's wife, were made members of the 25-member Central Committee.

At this point two things disturbed Mao. One was the deification of himself that Lin Piao had fostered during the three years of the Cultural Revolution. Lin had argued that it was necessary in order to secure support from the people. Mao had gone along, but personal glorification of this type was against his principles. Also he considered it a mistake, because he well knew that no one could avoid making mistakes. The idea that Mao Tse-tung was infallible, and that the thoughts expressed in the famous little red books were the ultimate truth, could react against him strongly when he did make mistakes.

Suspicious of everyone now, since so many of his old comrades-in-arms had chosen to put their own ambitions ahead of Party welfare, Mao wondered if Lin Piao was deliberately building the Mao image to the point where no man could live up to it. Then Lin could take advantage of future Mao mistakes to destroy the Chairman's image when it suited Lin's political ambitions to do so.

Lin certainly had ambitions to succeed Mao. He made no secret of this. Early in the Cultural Revolution Lin demanded, as the price of his indispensible services, that the Chinese Constitution be changed to name him Mao's successor as Party chairman. This was done at the 1969 Party Congress.

The action officially made Lin Piao the Party's number two man, downgrading Chou En-lai to third place.

With Lin Piao revealing his power ambitions in this way, Mao now had to consider the problem of how long Lin would be content to wait for Mao's natural death in order to move into first place. Assassination of Mao would not be out of character for a man of Lin Piao's past record.

Despite the internal turmoil of these years, China continued to progress economically. On the international front, conditions worsened with Russia but improved world-wide as more governments gave diplomatic recognition to the Chinese government. Since the outbreak of the Korean War the United States had led a long, successful fight to keep Red China out of the United Nations. This fight was finally lost in October, 1971, when the United Nations voted to admit the People's Republic of China and expel Nationalist China from China's seat in the Security Council.

At the same time there was a thawing in the icy relations between the United States and China, climaxed by a visit to Peking by President Richard M. Nixon in February, 1972.

For months previous to Nixon's visit there had been speculation that Mao was either sick or dead, but at the conclusion of Nixon's talks with Chou En-lai the American president was received by Mao. The resulting photographs showed him looking hale and hearty. Although he was then 79 years old, his talk with Nixon indicated that Mao was in full possession of his faculties and had not lapsed into senility, as Chu Teh had done.

There is no question that Mao Tse-tung, despite his advanced years, is still the dominating figure in the Chinese government. The former number two man, Lin Piao, died in an airplane crash in September, 1971. The crash was announced by Peking, but after that there was a strange silence that was not broken until July, 1972, when the Chinese embassy in Algiers released a story that Lin Piao, along with his wife and son, had died when their plane crashed in Mongolia

President Nixon shakes hands with Mao during Nixon's historic trip to China in February, 1972. *Wide World Photos.*

as they fled from Red China after Lin was accused of a plot to kill Mao Tse-tung.

"Lin Piao committed errors repeatedly, and Chairman Mao Tse-tung had time and again battled against him," the statement said.

"Outwardly he declared openly his support of the thought of Mao Tse-tung and made propaganda in favor of this thought. Thus he was able to hoax the masses of people into becoming in their eyes the 'successor' of Mao Tse-tung."

The startling announcement in Algiers was followed by confirmation from the Chinese embassy in Paris. A short time later, Mao himself told visiting French Minister Maurice Schumann that Lin had tried to assassinate Mao in order to replace the civilian government with his own military dictatorship.

Then in August, 1972, the *People's Daily* in Peking, which always reflects the official view, hinted that Lin Piao's plot against the government had been supported by Soviet Russia. Chen Po-ta, who had been involved in launching the Cultural Revolution with Lin Piao and Mao, was also said to have been involved in the plot.

Today Mao lives quietly in the Palace of the Fragrant Concubine, inside the old Forbidden City of the Manchus. He also has a mountain villa, where he goes sometimes when the summer heat stifles Peking. He continues to write and work, but this is mainly on policy and theoretical communism. The day-to-day business of the government is under the direction of Chou En-lai.

Chou is only four years younger than Mao. Eventually both men must be replaced. At the present time there is no indication who their successors will be, nor can anyone guess what turn Chinese politics will take when Mao is gone.

It is no secret that Russia believes she can again dominate Chinese Communism after Mao dies. Mao in turn was quoted recently as expressing fear that rightist elements in China will gain the upper hand when he dies. "Rightists" to Mao are those who want to deviate from the Maoist line. This line is his own deviation from Marxism and it is rigid and apparently unchanging. Quotations in the little red book going back to 1927 are still as pertinent to Mao's thought today as they were when they were first written.

It might be argued that the thaw in the cold war between China and the United States is an example of changing Mao's original thought, but this is not true. The little red book contains a quotation of sixteen years ago that gives authority for the presently improving relations between China and the United States.

It must be borne in mind that China suffered grievously at the hands of foreign nations for several hundred years. She can hardly be expected to believe that human nature, international politics and national interests have really undergone much change in the past thirty years.

With this in mind Mao wrote the following good advice for the Chinese people. It is also excellent advice for the people of the United States, and for the people of any other country that deals diplomatically with the People's Republic of China:

"As for the imperialist countries, we should unite with their peoples and strive to coexist peacefully with those countries, do business with them and prevent possible war, but under no circumstances should we harbor any unrealistic notions about them."

Appendix

MAJOR DATES IN THE LIFE OF MAO

1883 December 26, Mao Tse-tung born in Shao Shan, Hunan Province

1904 October, eleven-year-old Mao first learns about revolution when Huang Hsing tries to capture Changsa.

1906 Mao, now thirteen, learns revolt can pay off when his threat to kill himself defeats his father.

1907 Mao is married, against his will, to an older bride chose by his father. He refuses to live with the "old woman."

1909 Sixteen-year-old Mao Tse-tung leaves home to attend school in Siang-Siang.

1911 Mao, in company with his friend Emi Siao, leaves Siang-Siang to attend school in Changsa.

October, 1911, Sun Yat-sen's revolution opens. Mao joins the rebel army.

December, Mao reads his first article on Socialism and is electrified.

1912 Mao is demobilized from the Army. After failing in a trade school for soapmakers, he returns to college where he spends the next six years.

1914 Mao and his friend Siao-yu form the Hsin Min Study Association. Mao is introduced to Communism by a friend who gives him a translation of *The Communist Manifesto*, written by Karl Marx and Friedrich Engels.

1917 Siao-yu and Mao spend part of their summer vacation roaming as beggars through Hunan.

1918 Mao rejects chance to go to Paris and remains in China to build up the Hsin Min Study Association, which he hopes to use as a future Communist base. He goes to Peking.

1919 Mao goes to Changsa to work as an agitator against the corrupt governor. His newspaper is quickly suppressed by the authorities.

1920 A local revolt overthrows the warlord of Hunan, and Mao is rewarded with a political position in the government. He marries Yang Kai-hui, the daughter of a former professor he and Siao-yu studied under. Siao-yu was also in love with her.

1921 June, Mao takes part in the formation of the Chinese Communist Party.

1923 Mao at odds with the Communist Party for some obscure reason.

1924 Mao works as a coordinator between the Chinese Communist Party and the Kuomintang Party of Dr. Sun Yat-sen.

1925 Mao angers Party leader Chen Tu-shiu by writing an article arguing that the peasant must be the base upon which a successful revolution can be launched.

1926 Chiang Kai-shek, following death of Sun Yat-sen, pulls off a *coup d'etat* that gives him control of the Kuomintang Party.

1927 April, Chiang Kai-shek suddenly turns on the Communists in Shanghai, slaughtering 700.
September, Mao leads an Autumn Harvest uprising among the peasants in Hunan. He is defeated badly and flees with a shattered army to Chingkanshan Mountain.

1928 January, Chu Teh leads uprising in Hunan. May, Chu Teh, defeated, leads army to Chingkanshan, where he and Mao Tsetung begin their long, fruitful association.

1929 April, Chiang Kai-shek wins battle to dominate Kuomintang Party and launches determined attacks on Communists.
December, Mao Tse-tung puts forth his views on guerrilla warfare at the Kutien conference.

1930 Mao and Chu Teh involved in battle for Changsa.
Chiang Kai-shek begins his first Red Bandit Extermination Campaign in December.
Mao's wife, Yang Kai-hui killed sometime in 1930. (Other accounts put her death in both 1927 and 1928.)

1931 Mao begins to develop strength and enlarge his holdings in Kiangsi, which become the major Communist soviet.
Chiang Kai-shek launches his second and third extermination campaign against the Communists

1932 Mao marries Ho Tzu-chen, his third wife.
Kiangsi soviet continues to grow.

1933 Chiang Kai-shek seeks German aid in planning his final two extermination campaigns. He begins building blockhouses and a "ring of steel" about Mao's Kiangsi soviet.

1934 January, Second All-China Soviet Congress convenes in Juichin, Mao's soviet capital. Mao is removed from his Party office and placed under house arrest. Situation in Kiangsi soviet rapidly becoming desperate.
October, Mao and the First Front Red Army under Chu Teh begin their famous Long March.

1935 January, Mao challenges the Party leadership at Tsunyi and emerges as Party Secretary.
May 30, Long Marchers cross the Tatu River bridge.
June, Mao meets Chang Kuo-tao's Fourth Front Army.
August, Chang Kuo-tao breaks with Mao and returns to Szechuan.
October, Mao and the First Front Army reach Shensi Province.

1936 Chiang Kai-shek arrested by the Young Marshal. Mao sends Chou En-lai to negotiate Chiang's release.

1937 July 7, Japan invades China, launching Sino-Japanese war.
September, Chiang and Mao agree to end the ten-year-old civil war and unite against the Japanese invaders. Red Army joins the Kuomintang Army as the Eighth Route Army.

1938 Mao remains in Yenan, devoting himself to politics and writing his treatise *On Protracted War*.

1941 Chiang Kai-shek treacherously tries to destroy the Communist New Fourth Front Army in Central China.
Japanese attack on Pearl Harbor brings the United States into the war, resulting in American aid to Chiang Kai-shek.

1945 Japanese surrender, ending World War II. Chiang Kai-shek tries to prevent any Japanese surrendering to the Communist forces.

August 28, at American urging, Mao flies to Chungking for a conference with Chiang Kai-shek.

1947 The Civil War resumes.

1949 January 31, Lin Piao captures Peking (Peiping).

March 25, Mao Tse-tung enters Peking.

October 31, Mao proclaims the People's Republic of China

December 16, Mao visits Moscow.

1950 June 24, Korean War opens.

November, Mao permits Lin Piao to intervene in the Korean War.

1952 Mao launches China's first Five Year Plan.

1954 Campaign to stamp out resistance to Communist rule, which resulted in 800,000 deaths, ends.

1957 April, Hundred Flowers Campaign begins.

June, disorders and excessive criticism causes abandonment of Hundred Flowers Campaign.

1958 Commune system begins.

1959 April, Liu Shao-chi deposes Mao.

1966 Cultural Revolution restores Mao to power.

1971 Lin Piao killed while fleeing from China after an abortive attempt to kill Mao.

October, 1971, China admitted to the United Nations, taking the Chinese seat occupied by Nationalist China.

1972 February, President Richard M. Nixon visits Red China, talks with Mao.

Bibliography

Edmonds, I. G., *Revolts and Revolutions*. New York, Hawthorn, 1966.

Edmonds, I. G., *Taiwan, the Other China*. New York, Bobbs-Merrill, 1971.

Edmonds, I. G., *Mao's Long March*. Philadelphia, Macrae Smith, 1973.

Goldston, Robert, *Rise of Red China, The*. New York, Bobbs-Merrill, 1967.

Isaacs, Harold R., *Tragedy of the Chinese Revolution*. Stanford, Stanford University Press, 1966.

Ken Ling, *Revenge of Heaven, The*. New York, Putnam's, 1972.

Lifton, Robert J., *Revolutionary Immortal*. New York, Random House, 1968.

MacFarquhar, Roderick, *100 Flowers Campaign*. New York, Praeger, 1960.

Payne, Robert, *Mao Tse-Tung*. New York, Dutton, 1950.

Robottom, John, *China in Revolution*. New York, McGraw-Hill, 1967.

Rue, John C., *Mao Tse-tung in Opposition*. Stanford, Stanford University Press, 1966.

Siao-yu (Siao Shu-chung), *Mao Tse-tung and I were Beggars*. Syracuse, Syracuse University Press, 1959.

Smedley, Agnes, *The Great Road*. New York, Monthly Review Press, 1956.

Snow, Edgar, *Red Star Over China*. New York, Random House, 1938.

Swartz, Benjamin I., *Chinese Communism and the Rise of Mao*. Cambridge, Harvard University Press, 1951. (Rev.) 1966.

Wilson, Dick, *The Long March, 1935*. New York, Viking, 1972.

Index

DATE DUE

NOV 1 1 1996			